Utter Antiquity

Duke Monographs in
Medieval and Renaissance Studies 13

UTTER ANTIQUITY

Perceptions of Prehistory in Renaissance England

ARTHUR B. FERGUSON

Duke University Press Durham and London 1993

Printed in the United States of America
on acid-free paper ∞
Library of Congress Cataloging-in-Publication Data
appear on the last printed page of this book.

Contents

	Introduction	1
1	Euhemerism: The Medieval Tradition	13
2	A Mind Divided	23
3	The Age of Myth	46
4	A Secular Alternative	61
5	The British History: The Problem of Legend	84
6	A Digression on Giants	106
7	"Poesie Historical"	114
	Conclusion and a Glance Ahead	134
	Notes	143
	Index	165

Introduction

The purpose of this study is to explore the historical consciousness of Renaissance England as it sought to penetrate the mists of that most distant antiquity where history all but loses itself in myth and legend and where the historical imagination must serve, by default, the function of interpretation. We now know a great deal about how English thinkers of the sixteenth and early seventeenth centuries perceived the documentable past, but we know relatively little about how they perceived the past that stretches beyond, except, of course, for the version preserved in the Bible. Such lack of knowledge is strange, too, because that very stretch of time meant a lot to people of that day. In it, in the various gentile versions of it as well as the biblical, in what we should nowadays call "prehistory," they sought the logical vanishing point for the perspective of history they were coming more and more to consider essential, not only to the completion of their picture of universal history but to their own orientation in an age of ever more evident change.

Part of the problem stems from the fact that despite an increasing tendency to think historically, and in particular to draw moral and legal arguments from origins and from antiquity as such, spokesmen for the period felt little incentive to make a fresh approach to the earliest times. As far as it went, the Bible provided them with a source of historical truth that, however condensed it might be, was so generally accepted as authoritative as for all intents to rule out any idea that there could be a "prehistory." And the myths and legends of the gentiles provided a supplementary source that was still for the most part taken for granted, a source not only satisfying in itself to minds notoriously capable of accepting divergent accounts, but useful for filling in where *historia sacra* remained cryptic or silent. But another reason for our limited understanding is that present-day scholars are more interested—

and understandably so—in the newer archaeological and anthropological approaches to prehistory. They tend to be more concerned with what the ancient myths meant to the ancients themselves, or in what universal meaning they may still be thought to contain, than in what historical significance they may have had for Renaissance readers.

As far as the classical mythology is concerned, the studies contained in this volume focus accordingly upon the historical sense of those who read the ancient myths rather than upon the myths themselves, or upon what they may then have signified—or may still signify—as the expression of something archetypical and timeless. Even though Renaissance readers undoubtedly valued the classical myths primarily as symbol and allegory, they were ready, up to a point, to take them for granted as a true, if poetically expressed, account of the earliest age. But only up to a point. Their attitude toward the mythic past reflects also a new element, a subtly pervasive skepticism that was the product not so much of philosophical inquiry as of a rising conflict between the will to believe and a stirring discontent with explanations that did not square with reason and experience.

Yet skepticism, like heresy, implies a prevailing orthodoxy. In order, then, to estimate, as far as the paucity of comment will permit, either the ground level of belief or the degree of deviation from it—or, perhaps most important, the precarious balance of ambivalence with which Renaissance English intellectuals were curiously, and largely unconsciously, content—the reader is asked to adopt, for the moment, a certain literalness of mind to which, as a possible student of mythology, he may be unaccustomed and to remember that euhemerism was still taken widely as fact, and to contemplate the simple possibility that when an author refers, without qualification, to Jupiter as a "man" he may have meant exactly what he said—even though he may also have realized that the things he read about the deified Jupiter's doings weren't necessarily so. What the historian has to deal with is not so much a contest between unqualified belief and unbelief as the ability of Renaissance minds to half-believe or believe in contradictory things. As Paul Veyne has remarked with reference to the not dissimilar case of the ancient Greeks, such half-belief is much like that of children, who believe that Santa brings toys and at the same time believe that the toys were put there by their parents, or of the

Dorzé of Ethiopia, who believe that the leopard is a Christian animal which respects the fast days of the Coptic church, yet are no less careful to protect their livestock on those occasions.[1]

The myth-history supposedly contained in the classical heritage was not, it should be noticed, confined to the *gesta deorum.* It comprised also accounts of the "first age" that did, after a fashion, square with reason and experience. The idea, also derived from classical courses, that man lived initially in caves and forests, not unlike brute beasts, scattered and lacking all things necessary to civilized living, and that he managed, by his own efforts and in response to necessity, slowly to rise to a state of comparative civility proved to be a myth more nearly in the modern sense of an inspiring vision—a pregnant hypothesis that, whatever its relationship might be to actual history, served so well to explain the past in relation to the present as to become in itself an integral element in historical thought. Though seldom given extended or formal expression, this myth—for the sake of brevity I shall be referring to it simply as "the cave myth"—was in fact better able than the fables of the pagan gods, better even than the biblical story, to place the problems of contemporary life in a temporal perspective that extended to the beginning of time. Both the pagan and the biblical traditions told rather of persons than peoples, of catastrophic inventions rather than the evolution of society. Critics of contemporary England, on the other hand, were becoming more than ever conscious of social change and of the impersonal forces affecting it. They were coming to recognize, that is, that society itself had a history apart from patriarchs and kings, and, with an implicit faith in the validating authority of origins and antiquity per se, they were ready to trace that history beyond recorded memory to a mythic past they were only beginning to question, to a primeval age they could recover only by imaginative projection from the observable fact that society had indeed changed and, for good or ill, had changed from the simple to the complex. Moreover, by bypassing both Genesis and the Hesiodic pantheon, the cave myth was able to support a humanistic and confessionally neutral perception of prehistory.

For the gods, demigods, and heroes of classical mythology, confessional neutrality was, of course, impossible. They had to make their peace as best they could with *historia sacra.* Though they retained euhemeristic credentials as historical figures, as founders and inventors, they were themselves rooted in the religions of antiquity. Biblical scholars of the later Renaissance were only too ready to draft them into service as elements in their own scheme of a divinely ordained universal chronology, even to the point of identifying them with the more respectably historical figures of the Mosaic tradition. Yet these figures of myth managed to maintain a life of their own in English thought. As long as they did not directly challenge sacred history, as long as their stories, however fabulous, were believed to contain a kernel of truth, as few writers of the period doubted, or even an arcane wisdom veiled in allegory—in short, as long as they continued, without risk of impiety, to serve the purposes of the historical imagination, the pagan deities were able to maintain a shadowy identity as personages of history. The remarkable popularity they still enjoyed depended, it is true, to a predominant extent on their extreme usefulness in symbolic and allegorical expression, but for that very reason their names retained a currency they might not otherwise have had in historical thought.

In their efforts to penetrate the mists of antiquity, English authors were not, however, limited to the sources of inspiration provided by either classical or biblical antiquity. They had an antiquity of their own, complete with mists enough to pique the curiosity of the most romantic searcher for origins—an antiquity, moreover, that touched their sensibilities as Englishmen far more immediately than did the myths of a more distant age. Since they are situated nearer to recorded history, the legends about the national origins obviously belong to a different category than the myths involving the early life of man, but the problems they presented are in some respect related. The ancient poets believed to have been the creators of the pagan myths, in a sense the creators of the gods themselves as historical figures, were all but reincarnated in the Celtic bards who first sang of Britain's legendary past and its eponymous heroes. Nor was that parallel lost upon Tudor observers. Criticism of the legendary history in fact cast a fresh light on the process of mythmaking, and on the crucial role of poets in it.

Examination of the role of poets, in turn, raised basic questions regarding the still unresolved conflict between poetry and history that continued to hold hostage the idea of historical truth, especially as it applied to those reaches of the past where the possibility of finding empirical evidence became less and less likely, and where the historically conditioned imagination had increasingly to serve the purposes of interpretation. Awareness of the part played by poets in interpreting the most distant past gave rise to that unnaturally fertile hybrid known to contemporaries as "poesie historical." At a time of uneasily shifting epistemological positions, that concept acted, though with limited success, as a bridge between history proper and the quasi-history of myth and legend.

In the course of whatever attention they gave to a time before "known" history, a few of the more perceptive observers of the past came to consider the ancient myth-history less as a historical source than as the expression of an age peculiarly characterized by expression in poetry and fable, of a stage, that is, in the evolution of civilization. This tendency is related to the unprecedented willingness of Renaissance thinkers to look to history not solely for the universal and unchanging values it was supposed to teach by example, but also for a temporal perspective that would explain the relation the present bore to a past different from it yet related to it in an ongoing process. As far as the most distant past is concerned, the resulting relativism becomes evident in an ability to accept the historical mythology as in itself a fact of history rather than as historical fact, and euhemerism as a characteristic of ancient religion rather than as a comment on the historicity of the pagan gods. By the same token, this relativist perspective shows up in the ability of a few select minds to recognize mythmaking as a historical process, and, more important still, as a process typical of a primitive age of myth.

The notion of a primitive stage in the history of civilization, whether conceived as truly primeval and savage or as merely prerational and poetic, was as related to a developmental view of human history as it was contrary to the various, and popular, evocations, both pagan and Christian, of an original Age of Gold. Yet, such was the Renaissance capacity for ambivalence that even the most perceptive interpreter of what he believed to be a primitive mentality was also convinced that an arcane wisdom, good for all time, lay beneath the allegories supposedly contained in the ancient fables. The perception of a primitive age as a phase in the emergence of civilization received fresh support, together with renewed implications of cultural relativity and social evolution, from reports of New World savagery. American Indians could be thought to exemplify all primitive peoples, even the Greeks in their early days, and to document the idea that primitive peoples represented the childhood of the human race. If all this made questionable anthropology, it nevertheless opened up exciting hypothetical vistas.

In dealing with the perceptions of prehistory entertained by English intellectuals of the premodern era, we are naturally dealing more with belief than with knowledge. At a time when archaeology was as yet in its infancy, when anyone contemplating the frontiers of history had to rely largely on literary sources, including the mythmakers themselves, and when tradition still weighed heavily on the mind, belief would appear to have been safe and skepticism in for a bad time. The will to believe long-standing traditions is always strong. During the transition from medieval England to early modern, with its social changes and subtly shifting values, it was especially strong. Even the most realistic of minds seem to have wanted to believe if only they could—if only, that is, more evidence remained that could survive the scrutiny of a newly critical historical scholarship. For the most part, however, their ability to entertain divergent views allowed them to escape into a state of happy ambivalence which, if it did nothing to solve problems, at least made them easier to live with. The degree of their belief then depended in each instance on which way the scales of ambivalence tipped.

For the most part, those who paid attention to the myths and legends remained only too willing to suspend disbelief. The threshold of credulity was bound to be relatively low in an age that accepted the miraculous as given, witchcraft as a reality, and magic as a shortcut to knowledge and power—an age that still read the ancient and medieval cosmographers, with their marvels and monsters, and travelers' tales that made the American aborigines seem, by comparison, only a bit eccentric.

One may well wonder how skepticism, let alone disbelief, could have made any headway at all under these circumstances. Yet it did. And it had things going for it, too. The historical sense, sharpened not only by humanist scholarship but by the efforts of controversialists to bring in the past to redress the balance of the present, ensured that traditions would be subjected, as never before, to critical examination, especially those that impinged most directly on contemporary interests. Skepticism naturally surfaced more often and matured more rapidly into disbelief the nearer the subject was to documentable history, and the more it consequently touched a sensitive nerve in the contemporary mind. As a result, more can be learned about the capacity for doubt from reactions to controversies over the legends that told of the nation's own origins than from responses to the ancient myths that were increasingly insulated from historical criticism by allegorical interpretation—much as were the figures of biblical tradition by exegetical literalism. Skepticism, moreover, gained a certain passive support from a neutral source. The myth of man's early existence in caves and forests allowed those who wished to establish a historical perspective in the farthest reaches of antiquity, but who preferred the evidence of experience, to circumvent the traditional myths of origin, with their personalized and fabulous tales, and so to arrive at a more reasonable picture of man's emergence from the caves and a greater understanding of the impersonal factors affecting it.

But skepticism remained for a long time at best an undercurrent in English thought. Never so formally critical as Continental writers of the ability of the human intellect to arrive at historical truth, English skeptics derived their doubts rather from a visceral distrust of explanations that did not accord with experience and common sense. And the nature and extent of their doubts was further obscured by a chronic and permissive ambivalence. Few, if any, doubted that beneath the ancient fables and legends lay a substratum of truth. And, though the language of euhemerism had become so deeply involved in literary tradition that it was able long to outlast any sincere belief in its literal meaning, euhemerism remained, well into the eighteenth century, the largely unchallenged formula for mediating between mythology and history. Slow to catch up with Continental scholarship, English scholars continued to be more interested in placing the euhemerized gods and demigods in some rational scheme of universal chronology than in asking what their stories might tell about the religion of antiquity. As for the reading public, it had little to go on but the works of neo-euhemerists who had apparently freed themselves even from those doubts about the historicity of the gods that had contributed to the ambivalence of their predecessors. Eventually, of course, such overconfident attempts to rationalize pagan myths gave way before a newer rationalism born of a more mature understanding of primitive cultures. One is left, however, with the feeling that, despite their ambivalence—perhaps, indeed, because of the flexibility it allowed them—the more perceptive minds of Renaissance

England were able to achieve a more realistic appraisal of the ancient history myths than were their immediate successors, inhibited as the latter were by their renewed faith in euhemerism as an explanatory device.

Any attempt to trace the perceptions Renaissance writers had of a prehistoric antiquity is likely to be at best a hazardous operation. Hard as it is for the historian to enter into the historical consciousness of an earlier era, it is doubly hard when the subject is one about which contemporaries were notoriously of two minds, and when they usually wrote about it only in bits and pieces. Referring primarily to the controversy over the legendary history of Britain, and speaking from bitter experience, William Camden was moved to ask, "Who is so skilfull as in this dark ocean of antiquity to struggle with time without splitting on the rocks?" The question might have applied even more appropriately to the history myths of Greco-Roman antiquity.

It could apply just as well to historians themselves, for their sources provide them with few unambiguous points of reference. It is especially hard to tell at what point the literal meaning gives way to the symbolic and allegorical. At some point, however, one begins to get the feeling that the traditional genealogy of the gods was being recited with about the same concern for historicity as critics of more recent times have sometimes brought to a discussion of, say, Shakespeare's characters. At some point one begins to sense that the balance has shifted irrevocably from myth as history more than half believed, to myth as symbol with no more than lingering echoes of a euhemerism no longer taken literally. One notices that the gods owe their remarkable longevity not to their historical credentials but to the congenial atmosphere of allegory, and that they remain of interest to historians primarily as data for the history of ancient beliefs. The historian, then, is bound at some point to stop and ask the direct question, Did Renaissance England really believe that the deities of classical antiquity were historical figures? The question may be too invidious to ask of a people for whom mythmaking was still a living mode of thought and poetic expression a more or less legitimate vehicle for historical interpretation. It is in any case a historian's question, not one that persons of that day would have been likely to ask, and it cannot be answered with a simple yes or no. Yet it must be asked, if only because, by making possible an educated guess as to the extent of commitment in this particular respect, something may be learned about the larger problem of historical consciousness in that peculiarly transitional period.

Other questions, not unrelated to the problem of belief, suggest themselves. As we have seen, historians will want to know to what extent authors of the Renaissance were able to contemplate the process of mythmaking as a fact of history, and accordingly as a legitimate subject for historical investigation. They will want to know whether these authors succeeded in visualizing an age in the development of civilization peculiarly characterized by the making of myths. They will want to know to what extent the idea of a primitive society translated into a recognition of social evolution.

Once beyond the classical myth-history, the historian's problem becomes, if not simpler, at least more conventional. Though derived initially from classical sources, the myth of man's rise from a stone-age existence, and as a result of his own reaction to necessity, is entirely free from the euhemerized inventors of pagan tradition and from the linguistic conventions that so long screened them from historical scrutiny. Imaginary as it had to be, the "cave myth" nevertheless represented a projection of experience and was relatively free from limiting theological considerations, whether pagan or Christian. As a result, it sets in motion an essentially human train of historical thought. In the case of the national legends, too, the historian does not have to go far beyond the frontiers of "known" history; and, in the light of controversy, the conflict between belief and skeptical rationalism stands forth in relatively clear outline. But the case of the British legends has its own ambiguities, for it raises the question, especially difficult for the modern mind to deal with, of the relationships between history and poetry. Since it relates also to the myth-history of classical antiquity, that question becomes all the more important.

In these studies I have accepted certain limitations—some for obvious reasons, others for practical purposes. Myth and legend, even when considered in the already limited role as the perceived purveyors of history, together constitute a subject so large as to be hard to digest as whole, and I have not had the temerity to try to do so. Nor have I attempted to cover all possible aspects of it even for England.

The studies have been limited to England. The case of England is, in the present context, to a significant extent unique. For one thing, the English authors on whom one must depend for evidence of historical consciousness were not, as a whole, especially interested in mythology per se—not, at any rate, before the seventeenth century when the relatively sophisticated work being done on the Continent in such areas as chronology and biblical criticism began to filter into England. This is not to mean that the classical heritage was neglected, or that its myth-history had lost its appeal for the English imagination. English readers knew their classical mythology, no doubt about that. Long familiar with Boccaccio's *Genealogia deorum,* after the mid-sixteenth century they read, and eventually translated or adapted, the elaborate manuals of Conti, Cartari, and Ripa.[2] But they remained largely content to rely on these outside sources and showed little critical interest in the ancient myths, other than as legal tender for literary exchange.

The intellectual atmosphere of Renaissance England was not, in fact, conducive to a systematic critique of the mythological tradition—nor, for that matter, to "pure" scholarship of any kind. English humanism, the steering force in English intellectual life for more than a century, might well have been expected to have provided motivation for a study so close to its own classical interests, but its attention was directed elsewhere. An essentially applied learning, it was preoccupied with the issues of contemporary England rather than with scholarship for its own sake. Yet in those respects, in the politico-ecclesiastical controversies, for example, authors so engaged in fact did more than conventional writers of history to sharpen the perception of historical process. Whereas historical scholarship in England responded quickly to current issues, including the patriotic issue raised by the controversy over the British legends, such historical implications as emanated from the classical myths remained too removed from the world of affairs to be seriously affected by its vicissitudes. It is no accident that Renaissance England found the most congenial source of inspiration in its classical heritage not in the *gesta deorum,* but in the impersonal anthropology of the "cave myth," with its heady suggestions of social evolution.

Although in many respects idiosyncratic, the attitudes of English scholars and writers-at-large toward prehistory cannot be evaluated in isolation from outside influences. Not only were those authors willing to rely heavily upon the work of Continental mythographers, but they relied upon those extensive treatments of cosmography and cultural history that customarily began at the beginning and were therefore most likely to have something worth noticing to say on the subject of the earliest age. It has therefore been necessary to make occasional use of these foreign authors who either lived for an extended time in England or whom the English themselves, as were their wont, adapted and translated and in one way or another made their own—such, for example, as Boemus, Vives, and LeRoy. Though generally sketchy enough on the earliest ages, works of this sort often serve to fill in the even sketchier native versions and to confirm the incidental references and *obiter dicta* on which the historian has only too often to rely when dealing with the perceptions of prehistory.

Students of the period will notice one major omission. In view of the fact that perceptions of prehistory in the Renaissance inevitably involved *historia sacra,* they may wonder especially why a separate study has not been devoted to it. The reason for this omission is that the biblical mythology, so far from being unimportant, is so pervasive a part of the historical thought of the time as to suggest dealing with it as it bore on other myths of origin rather than by itself. The account in Genesis of man's early history was then so generally taken for granted that it can also safely be taken as given in the present context except where there is a need to explain other perceptions of prehistory. Although the studies contained in this volume tend to highlight the secular element in sixteenth- and seventeenth-century English thought, that element has in fact constantly to be defined in relation to the theological.

The first of the following studies deals with the problem of euhemerism, the problem fundamental to any investigation of the history supposedly contained in the ancient myths, as it matured during the later Middle Ages. Moderated by the undoctrinaire rationalism that persistently crops up in the writings of fourteenth- and fifteenth-century England, this version of euhemerism seemingly left little for succeeding generations to do, and in fact it continued, in one degree or another, to shape thought on the subject throughout the Renaissance and well beyond. The inadequacies nevertheless inherent in euhemerism as an explanatory device, and the consequent emergence of skepticism tempered by ambivalence, become the subjects treated in the next chapter. The third study deals with the emerging ability and willingness of certain commentators, under the combined influence of skeptical rationalism and humanist historical scholarship, to concern themselves not so much with euhemerism—which they were coming in any case to consider in relation more to ancient religion than to the historicity of the pagan gods—as with the process of mythmaking itself and with its significance as a characteristic of a particular age in the history of civilization. The next two chapters examine two perceptions of prehistory that have little or nothing to do with the classical fables. Chapter four deals with "the cave myth," the myth of man's earliest existence in caves and forests and his subsequent struggle toward a state of comparative civility, and with the seminal implications that emanate from it in the direction both of historical perspective and an experiential view of universal history. In chapter five, the emphasis shifts from ultimate myths of origin to the legends about national origins that lay close enough to recorded history to become the subject of serious, if more often than not misguided, scholarly debate. The last chapter picks up the problem of poetic history for which the preceding one has provided something of a case study. It is concerned especially with the attempt of Renaissance critics to find in poetic expression a means of mediating between the vision of the past preserved in myth and legend and a perspective that could reasonably be made to accord with historical scholarship—an attempt that, though it misfired, helped nonetheless to clarify the nature of historical interpretation.

I

Euhemerism: The Medieval Tradition

Whatever the problems involved in the "footsteps of history" discernible to Renaissance authors in the ancient myths, they have to be dealt with in the context of the euhemerist tradition. It was a tradition that proved remarkably adaptable and durable. In the third century B.C. Euhemerus himself had satisfied the naturalistic instincts never far from the surface of Greek culture by popularizing the idea that the gods had once been mortals deified by a grateful people for some signal service; and the idea continued to satisfy those in later centuries who, for one reason or another, likewise preferred to explain the gods in quasi-historical terms rather than as fantasies born of fear or favor. Palaephatus, his successor as a prophet of euhemerism, showed how obviously fabulous elements in the historical fables could be explained away, leaving standing a true history. And Diodorus Siculus, whose universal history, though pagan, enjoyed a considerable currency in the early church, went one step further than Palaephatus by retelling the stories of the gods as though they were chapters in the history of the world.[1]

Euhemerism continued well beyond the Renaissance years to provide the most popular means of reconciling ancient myth and history. Like other paradigms that have outlived their usefulness, it received its most vigorous defense when it was no longer taken for granted. Eighteenth-century English readers were still indulging their curiosity about the gods and the early history of man, of which they were supposed to be a part, by reading Antoine Banier's enormously influential work, Englished as *Mythology and Fables of the Ancients Explain'd from History* (1739–40), which contained as unblinking a statement of euhemerism as was ever made, and one, moreover, that reflected eminently respectable contemporary scholarship, including that of England's own Samuel Shuckford and William Warburton, as well as of Sir Isaac Newton in his less scientific moments. Granting that knowledge of mythology is useful and necessary as an adjunct to polite learning the good abbé insisted that "what makes Mythology still of greater importance, and at the same time gives it a greater claim to be the Object of our Curiosity, is to consider, that Fables were not mere Fictions, . . . but that most of the Gods had been Men, whose History makes a part of the particular Nations from whom they had divine Honour." And he castigated contemporary scholarship for failing to unfold the origin of the gods, for failing to "distinguish those Gods who are often the same under different Names," and for burying the history they do document "under a heap of Allegory and arbitrary Moralizing."[2] It was, of course, that very heap of arbitrary moralizing that had kept mythology alive long after its historical meaning had begun to run terminally thin. Yet the fact remains that euhemerism continued for a remarkably long time to provide a much-needed and seemingly rational support for the historical imagination as it coped with prehistory.

Useful as the euhemerist formula may have been in mediating myth and history, it did not, of course, necessarily imply historicity. That ancient peoples often deified great men is a fact of history, but it does not follow that the gods were in fact ex-mortals or even that they existed outside the imagination of the poets who sang of them. As Mircea Eliade has pointed out, the collective memory of archaic peoples can retain historical concepts only as they are transformed into archetypes that escape the strictures of historical time and live on in the infinite recurrence of ritual.[3] The euhemerizing process was capable of creating just such archetypes rather than commemorating specific human beings. As archetypal figures, the pagan deities, like the figures of Christian typology, transcend historical time. As a matter of fact, however, the pagan gods entered into medieval thought, and even into the more historically oriented thought of Renaissance England, both as archetypical figures more at home in allegory than history and as historical personages whose credentials were underwritten by the euhemerist tradition. Jupiter, for example, could be taken seriously as a personage of history, a king of Crete, with an actual birthplace that Juan Luis Vives tells us had become by his day something of a tourist attraction,[4] yet, when next met with, he might appear rather as a symbolic figure, a general-purpose god. Or, to take an example from the ranks of the fabled heroes, Hercules could be given a circumstantially human biography but was readily transmuted into the archetypical man of might, the slayer of monsters, the figure with whom ambitious Renaissance monarchs could, and did, proudly identify. In the process of moving from quasi-historical personage to archetype, both god and hero suffered a fragmentation of whatever historical identity tradition had afforded them, with the result that anyone who took euhemerism as a guarantee of historicity had often to contend with a multiplicity of deities known by the same name.

Nevertheless, when a respectable Renaissance humanist, in the course of scholarly writing, identifies Jupiter as "a man, mighty and wise,"[5] one is justified in assuming that he meant what he said. Or when an author recounts the story of Saturn's career after he had taken refuge in Italy as circumstantially as he would the story of the siege of Troy or the exploits of Alexander, one may presume that he is stating what he took to be a historical account. But even then one has to remember that the truth of history had not yet been clearly distinguished in Renaissance England from the other truth of fiction as preserved in the poetic imagination.[6] Perhaps we can only be sure that the gods are being taken historically when they appear linked with the biblical personages of unquestioned historicity in a universal chronology.

Despite obvious limitations as a device for explaining prehistory, euhemerism remained a concept inevitably involved in historical time. It provided a convenient shortcut to the historical problems involved in the rise of civilization, and at a time when the longer road was not yet clearly marked, but the notion of invention it fostered was far too personalized and catastrophic to satisfy the awareness of social evolution emerging in Renaissance thought.[7] Yet euhemerism performed a service of sorts in keeping the pagan myths in at least imaginary touch with history, thus, for good or ill, preventing their being relegated entirely to the ahistorical category of allegory. Insofar as euhemerism involved an imaginary vision of history, moreover, it was a thoroughly human one. By explaining pagan divinity in human terms, it appealed to the preference, increasingly apparent in the later Middle Ages and Renaissance, for viewing human problems in the light of experience,[8] much as it had appealed to the naturalistic temper of the ancient Greeks. In this context, euhemerism, in its turn, gained an enhanced respectability. Even those who professed to deplore the ancient myths as relics of paganism and seeds of idolatry felt obliged to make them as believable as possible in human terms. By explaining away the fabulous and monstrous element in the fables, such efforts tended to leave the euhemerized gods standing on seemingly solid historical grounds.

Though ambivalent about the gods, the medieval church was in fact instrumental in maintaining the euhemerist tradition. Its spokesmen found it wonderfully convenient to believe that the gods, of whom they basically disapproved, were really men and women like any others in history—bad enough that they were pagan, worse that they were all too human, worst of all that worship of them fostered the odious practice of idolatry. Yet they could not help admiring the gods as inventors, as culture heroes; and, in view of the extremely sketchy treatment given that aspect of man's early life in the Bible, they found their stories useful for filling out a coherent scheme of universal history. The church quickly recognized that the fables, allegorically interpreted, even more useful as moral philosophy teaching by example, and, as such, provided a valuable supplement to Christian teaching. The gods themselves thus tended to live dual lives.

Euhemerism may, indeed, have thrived, as it did during the later Middle Ages, less because of its merits as history than because it lent verisimilitude to allegorical interpretation. Certainly it enjoyed something of a symbiotic relationship with allegory. Viewed in the light of euhemerism, the fables provided a virtually inexhaustible source of persuasively human materials for the allegorist, and the allegorist, as moral philosopher, lent a reflected respectability to the euhemerized gods.

To understand how Renaissance England perceived the historical element in the classical myths, one must begin with those late medieval authors who recognized the problem of mythical history so clearly as, it would at first glance seem, to leave little for their successors to do. It was a time more conducive to the study of classical mythology than any since the patristic period. If the classics were not yet being read clearly in the perspective of history, they were to an ever increasing extent being read. In the early fourteenth century, Ralph Higden, the "classicizing monk,"[9] had already used, directly or indirectly, most of the pagan authors then available, as well as his favorite Christian apologists Augustine and

Isidore, and had woven the mythical figures into the broad and ragged tapestry of his "universal" history. Despite their disapproval of pagan religion, these authors of late medieval England rehearsed the genealogy of the gods with undiminished enthusiasm and in terms circumstantially euhemeristic.

Euhemerism, indeed, served for Higden and his successors as a ready-made philosophy of secular history, as well as a useful supplement to *historia sacra.* Of the triumvirate of late medieval English poets, Gower and Lydgate, but oddly enough not Chaucer, saw fit to insert euhemeristic digressions into their massive poetical works.[10] Lydgate, for example, saw Saturn as "wilom the might kyng of Crete," falsely called "god of goddes alle" and given ultimately the name of a planet.[11] In his adaptation of LeFèvre's *Recuyell of the Historyes of Troye,* William Caxton created a highly romanticized and curiously anachronistic but thoroughly human version of the Hesiodic pantheon, in which he pictured the antique gods not only as actual rulers and inventors but as knights organizing tournaments on Mount Olympus.[12]

Euhemerism, however, by its very nature, engendered ambivalence. The poets who first sang the humanity of the gods were themselves only too human, and much given to the spinning of tall tales. Those who accepted their interpretation, yet shared the impulse toward rationalization increasingly apparent in late medieval writings, had therefore a nagging problem. They had somehow, and to some extent, to draw a line between the supposedly historical element in the fables and the obviously fabulous. They had, that is, to assess what they customarily referred to as the "feigning" of the "poets." But for people still only too willing to suspend disbelief when presented with miracles and tales of monsters, marvels, and chimeras, people who could read the ethnological lore of the encyclopedists or the travels of Sir John Mandeville without blinking, to do so was not likely to result in a cognitive revolution. Medieval authors knew well enough that history was supposed to differ from fiction, but they had difficulty in finding any clear line of demarcation. Nor were they always strongly motivated to look for it, given the didactic value that clung to the ancient fables and the symbiotic relationship that existed between euhemerism and allegory. Higden clearly worried about it at times, but Christine de Pisan, whose *mythologia,* Englished as *The Epistle of Othea to Hector,* was familiar to English readers, was so devoted to the task of teaching by the example of the gods that it is impossible to tell what, if anything, she thought about their historicity.

Assessing the "feigning" of poets is not easy for the historian either. To "feign," according to modern usage, means to tell something that is simply not true—to imagine, to pretend. In premodern parlance it is not so strictly limited. It could fall somewhere between truth and falsehood, imaginative but with the saving grace of verisimilitude. And, before the rise of a scholarship devoted to documentary authenticity, or a puritanical tendency to dismiss all imaginative literature as "lies," verisimilitude—the kind of truth-to-the-life that may be historical without being factual—could support an extension of the historical vision beyond the range of documentable fact. To this extent the prehistory of mankind continued to depend on the feigning of poets.

There are signs that a few minds in late medieval England were ready if not to doubt the truth of the myth-history as a whole—they were all basic euhemerists—at least to recognize that the fables did pose a problem of truth. A current of commonsense realism is detectable in the atmosphere of the time. A climate that could foster Sir John Fortescue's realistic ideas on the governance of England, Reginald Pecock's insights into the history of the church as a human agency, Sir Thomas Malory's willingness to rationalize and historicize the Arthurian legends, and Caxton's somewhat confused hope that "history" might be distinguished from "fable" could be expected to have taken the problem of feigning seriously. It was Higden, however, who gave it most thought, and who left, in his *Polychronicon,* a model treatment of it to the generations of English readers who continued to go to that work for their conception of universal history.

Higden found himself continually frustrated by the admixture of the obviously fabulous with what, on the authority of his respected classical and patristic authors, he took to be fact. He could, for example, accept Jupiter as a great prince but not his being transformed into the likeness of a bull.[13] And as he tried to weave the debatable history contained in the myths of ancient Greece into the given fabric of biblical narrative, he ran into some confusing tangles—more than one Mercury, for example, and a number of Herculeses.[14] His authors were of some help to him on that score. Augustine had noticed that a variety of men, including the biblical Sampson, had been called Hercules simply because they shared his attribute of strength exerted in the common interest. But not all discrepancies were so readily resolved. Higden apparently found the problem of distinguishing fact from fable so basic that he decided to devote a special chapter to it.[15] The result comes as close as any medieval English writing ever came to a philosophy of history-in-myth—if, that is, it is cricket to inject some degree of order into what reads like the jumble of notes which it undoubtedly was.

Higden believed that fables were of three kinds, involving varying degrees of "falsehood": those, like Aesop's, intended to exhort the people—which is simply falsehood embodied in falsehood ("hoc est falsum per falsum"); those, as Hesiod's on the gods, meant to render a true story in fictitious terms, which then becomes not a fable but a fabulous narration ("non fabula sed fabulosa narratio"); and those, such as the story of Scipio's dream about the immortality of the soul, that are totally "feigned," but for justifiably philosophical purposes. The fabulous element itself had a history. It had been interjected by poets during a period located somewhere between the death of Joshua and the Trojan War. Although the concept of "fable" was not necessarily pejorative, any more than that of "poet," Higden, like his favorite, Isadore, all but identified "fables" with "lies" ("mendaciae"); and he seems to have felt somehow betrayed by the poets like Homer who, according to the Sybil's prophecy, was to write "lies" about the fall of Troy.[16] In any case, it was not always easy to tell the true from the fabulous. Many myths were so obviously contrary to common sense as to be fabulous in any use of the word, or at the very least "poetical"—the aerial exploits of Daedalus and Icarus, for example, or Amphion's famous drawing of stones to himself by the sweetness of his harp. Others could be seen to have arisen out of fact: the idea that men were born of stones and trees after a great flood could be explained by the then uncontested belief that people in those days did indeed live in hollow trees as well as caves. Then there were cases where, though the story itself might be false, truth might be found in its significance. Higden could not accept as true that, according to the Romans, Aeneas was born of the goddess Venus and Romulus of the god Mars (he had Varro to vouch for him on this), yet he noted that it is politically useful for men of nobility to think of themselves as descended from gods, even if it is not true, and for ordinary citizens to find inspiration in a reflected glory.

Higden's efforts to separate fact from fancy reveal not so much a naturally skeptical mind as a desire to rationalize the historical record, to humanize it.[17] He seems to have wanted to believe, but, bedeviled by discrepant accounts, he had at best to reserve judgment. He warned his readers at the outset not to believe everything they read, and he was moved at one point to declare that "there is no lie so shameless that it is entirely without corroborating witness."[18] On the pagan mythology, in particular, he had apparently absorbed enough of Augustine's skepticism (if not the Gilbertian mood of his critical attacks on the Roman gods with their unseemly jostling for jurisdiction) to keep his euhemerism within reasonable bounds.[19]

Higden's skepticism may have been more borrowed than spontaneous. Certainly it reflects that of his sources. But it can be read also in the light of the realism that characterizes much late medieval English writing. And, since the *Polychronicon* remained for generations of English readers the standard textbook of world history, the attitude of its author toward the classical fables, original or not, could hardly help being transmitted to readers no doubt more ready than he to take a commonsense approach to such things. In the prologue to his edition of the *Polychronicon,* Caxton took pains to distinguish the didactic element in the classical mythology from historical fact—"the terrible feigned Fables of Poets," which nevertheless moved men to pity and justice, from "the ancestress of verity" and "the mother of all philosophy."[20]

Euhemerism served not only to bring the pagan deities into the scheme of human history, but to explain how and why that process had taken place. Inquiring minds in late medieval England became interested in this aspect of euhemerism not as humanists before their time, nor necessarily as admirers of the mythological tradition, but as men who saw the rise of idolatry as a major turning point in human history. The "poets," they saw, had not only fabricated the fabulous stuff of pagan myth, they had, in a very real sense, created the gods.

This realization was eventually to erode belief in the literal historicity of the gods beyond recovery, and it came as near doing so in late medieval writings as it was again to do until well into the Renaissance era. Higden himself had found plenty of authority for poets as creators of the gods in his patristic and classical sources.

Augustine, he noted, had traced to poets the whole hierarchy of gods, demigods, and heroes.[21] According to other authorities, poets either had for self-serving motives given the names of actual people to the various functions in terrestrial life, or (bypassing the euhemeristic process entirely) had, as an intellectual convenience, merely invented the names and actions of gods "to fit the various natures and qualities of things."[22] Lydgate, who expressed so well what oft was thought in early fifteenth-century England, tied idolatry directly to euhemerism: "For some Saturn 'god of godes all' / Gan in their error falsely for to call, / That was whilom the mighty King of Crete."[23] The author of *Assembly of Gods,* a poem at one time attributed to Lydgate, professed to see in the machinations of the poets a pious fraud. Though they had at first "feigned many a fable / To discrete reason right acceptable," poets later on enhanced their stories for popular consumption—"in this said time the people was so rude"—by fitting them with the names of notable men whom they got the populace, "deceived by ignorance," to think of as gods. Thus arose idolatry, for simple people took literally what poets expressed "under cover of fable."[24]

By bringing into focus an aspect of euhemerism that lent itself especially to explanation in terms of human nature, the problem of idolatry gave a peculiar immediacy to the mythmaking, god-creating process. According to medieval tradition, derived initially from the Book of Wisdom, idols arose in the course of veneration paid to a deceased king or relative.[25] The most frequently repeated account told of Ninus, who in his grief made an image of his dead father to which he then paid divine honors. Others, however, followed suit, and soon a custom began to take shape. What began as an understandable human folly in time degenerated into the worship of images dedicated to newly created gods.[26]

Reginald Pecock dissented—as was his wont—but rested his case still more firmly on assumptions about human nature.[27] In an effort to counter Lollard condemnation of the use of images in contemporary churches, he undertook a speculative reconstruction of religious life in those earliest communities that lived by reason alone, unsupported by divine revelation. He found in human nature a universal impulse to discover a god of some sort, but, following Hermes Trismegistus rather than the Apocrypha, and aided by his own reason—by which he meant something akin to the historical imagination—he preferred to explain early polytheism and the idolatry to which it led not as the deification of great men, but as a reaction to the awe inspired in simple souls by the mystery of the heavenly bodies. On the assumption that, as spiritual forces, the stars could affect terrestrial life, they came to be worshiped as gods. Idolatry thus arose naturally out of the very human need to give concrete form to the object of worship, to have, in other words, something tangible with which to associate spiritual things, something with which to identify.

Though too radical to be typical, Pecock's rationalism shows how such thinking could undermine euhemerism as an explanation of pagan religion, and his emphasis on the psychological meaning of idolatry left the pagan gods not too far from the position to which modern scholarship has relegated them. True, his was in some respects a Janus-headed mind. His rationalism points to the future, yet it remained essentially the rationalism of the late medieval schools. The freshness that is clearly reflected in it is a function of his humanism, but his humanism is the product of a native sense of man's ability, under God, to shape his own customs and institutions to suit his needs, and remains innocent of the newer humanism then beginning to seep into England from Italy. Pecock stands rather for the undoctrinaire realism stirring in later medieval English thought, a mind-set by no means congenial to euhemerism.

As seen in the diverse examples cited in the preceding pages, euhemerism was already undergoing subtle changes in emphasis. Though a skeptical heir to a skeptical tradition, Higden still had no choice but to take the deified men and women of pagan tradition as historical figures. Lydgate and whoever wrote *Assembly of Gods,* on the other hand, were able, in effect if not by intent, to focus attention on euhemerism as a process and to present it as in itself a fact of history, thus leaving the gods to what was clearly felt to be their primary duty as allegorical personae, without specifically calling into question their right to exist in history. And Pecock's rationalism allowed him to achieve anthropological insights that in effect reduced, if they did not deny, the importance commonly ascribed to euhemerism as an explanation of pagan religion. Together these men reflect the latent and too often unsuspected originality of late medieval English thought, humanist before humanism in its willingness to explain things human in human terms.

2
A Mind Divided

Having read the comments on the historicity of the pagan gods made by later medieval authors, the reader may justifiably wonder what, other than outright denial, they left for their Renaissance successors to do. Such an impression would, it is true, be hard to square with changes known to have been taking place in the climate of thought. Yet attitudes toward the inherited myth-history were slow to show the effects of those changes. To the extent that the myths were irrelevant to the forces affecting historical thought and congenial to those affecting literary and symbolic expression, they were largely insulated from those currents in contemporary culture most damaging to their credibility as an extension of history. Mythmaking was still a living mode of thought in Renaissance England, nor had history as yet freed itself entirely from poetry and the truth of the imagination.[1] Minds accustomed to accepting without serious question the myth-history contained in Genesis had little reason for rejecting the same contained in the pagan myths on any other ground than that they were pagan. For the most part, in fact, euhemerism was taken for granted as the basic formula for reconciling pagan myth and history. The fact remains, however, that Renaissance thinkers of all calibers were becoming accustomed, as never before, to historical modes of thought, and, as never before, felt either a rationalistic urge to make believable the unbelievable or an equally rationalistic urge toward skepticism. Little wonder, then, that whatever evidence there is concerning the historicity of the gods remains curiously equivocal.

It is certainly easy enough to document the conservatism of English attitudes toward the classical history myths during the sixteenth and early sventeenth centuries. If we are to take the representative spokesmen at their word—as we must, up to a point, even granting the inertia of conventional language—Renaissance Englishmen still for the most part took it for granted that the gods, demigods, and heroes of classical mythology were initially real people, no matter how abstracted they may have become in the process of apotheosis and, still more so, in the service of allegory. Sir Thomas Elyot, as enlightened as any of the early Tudor humanists, had no trouble describing Jupiter in his presumably factual dictionary as "a man, mighty and wise."[2] Almost a century later, George Sandys, the interpreter of Ovid to Jacobean England, is still declaring unequivocally that "Neptune was a mortal (as the rest of the gods)."[3] Nor did the English men of letters who adapted the work of the great Continental mythographers for domestic consumption depart markedly from the euhemeristic assumptions, or from the traditional language, of their sources. And Sir Walter Ralegh seems at first glance to have differed little in his conception of the ancient gods from that of his predecessor as England's "universal" historian, Ralph Higden. The pagan gods, moreover, were still borrowing collateral support from more or less scholarly efforts to incorporate them, along with the sacrosanct figures from Scripture, in a single time scheme. Ralegh had not more doubt than had Higden that such a universal chronology was possible, and we find him trying to place his various Jupiters in it, and locating Prometheus in "about the time of Moses."[4]

The ancient fables would seem indeed to have appeared as historical to most Elizabethans readers as they had been to medieval ones. They remained in any case the only commonly available source for the prehistory of pagan antiquity. As one versifier put it, should the "stories" be forgotten,

> No wit would work a way by pen to show
> The state of such as lived long ago.[5]

Even the national legends seemed unable to escape the domination of the classical myths. Those authors—Michael Drayton, Thomas Heywood, and William Warner—who undertook to popularize the history of England still felt called upon to begin their treatment of it with Saturn and the Hesiodic pantheon.[6]

Yet the appearance of continuity is deceptive. It masks a growing willingness to question anything that did not bear the stamp of sacred history, to rationalize where possible, and to historicize. Likening Ralegh to Higden, though provocative, ignores fundamental differences between them, and much more than the obvious difference in their learning and worldly experience. Higden, it is true, had his own share of skepticism, and it was sincere enough as far as it went, but its substance was largely borrowed from antiquity—from Varro via Augustine, or from Augustine himself, or from Cicero—and it had to do mostly with discrepancies among his classical sources. Ralegh's was nourished by the commonsense realism of a man who, despite a curious weakness for tales of strange and monstrous peoples, knew the real world far better than did the medieval monk who had probably never been farther than fifty miles from his house, and his threshold of credulity was immeasurably higher.

Elizabethan Protestants may have been no more ready than medieval Catholics to forgive the "poets" for deifying mortals, and just as ready to link euhemerism to idolatry, but their prejudice came at times close to outright disbelief in the literal truth of ancient fable. In the preface he wrote for his translation of Cartari, Richard Lynche declares that "the matter itself" is "wholly fictitious," and he altered the title, Englished as *The Image of the Gods,* to read *The Fountaine of Ancient Fictions* (1599). Stephen Batman, too, appears to give just as little credence to the "putative and imagined Gods of the Gentiles."[7] True, both gentlemen may seem to protest too much: the gods still appear in their pages in traditional euhemerist guise. Nevertheless, this willingness on the part of properly religious writers to treat the fables as indeed fabulous and to call them "fictions" surely tended to sap the historical essence from their underlying euhemerism.

Neither were the national legends immune from questioning. As we shall see in a later chapter,[8] the British legends became the subject of a prolonged and bitter controversy. If their heroes were scarcely demigods, they served in an analogous capacity and traced their lineage ultimately to both biblical and classical sources. If Drayton clung tenaciously to the medieval tradition in his ambitious poetical history, John Selden, reflecting a newer and more rigorous scholarship, provided a counterbalance in the at times mischievous notes he was persuaded to write for the poem on the understanding that, since the author was writing poetry, he must be given a poet's license. Much of the story, he said, was no more "warrantable" than "Ariosto's narration of persons and places in his

Rowlands, Spenser's elfin story, or Rabelais his strange discoveries."[9] And he spoke with scorn of "the whole chaos of Mythic invention."[10]

Furthermore, English intellectuals were not being left entirely to their own devices in this, as in so many other matters. In addition to the relatively sophisticated study of chronology being carried on in Europe—which, if it did little to undermine belief in the historicity of the gods, at least introduced an element of order into English discussions affecting it[11]—cooler breezes were blowing from abroad bearing suggestions of a human history to which the gods were irrelevant. Jean Bodin, for example, whose work was apparently well known in late Renaissance England,[12] virtually ignored the pagan history myths in his discussion of the method and meaning of history, referring to them only to demolish the traditional notion of the Four Ages: how foolish to ground belief in postdeluvian ages of gold and silver on the monstrous legends of the Greek gods.[13] And Louis LeRoy, whose *De la vicissitude* was equally familiar to English readers, left no place at all in his introductory account of early man for the Greco-Roman deities except as symbols.[14]

It is not hard to document a current of skeptical rationalism potentially damaging to the euhemeristic interpretation of the history myths. Yet the crisis of belief in Renaissance England is not so easily disposed of. Erosion of belief in the historicity of the pagan gods becomes apparent not so much in outright expressions of disbelief or skepticism as in a typically Renaissance state of ambivalence. Disbelief seldom stands alone in English writings of the period, nor is it safe to isolate skepticism from a context still generally conservative. The Renaissance mind, forced to mediate a process of radical transition, is in any case notorious for its ability to find truth in opposites and in apparently contradictory arguments, to say nothing of its immoderate taste for paradox. In the case of the myth-history, it is true, ambivalence was hard to avoid. The gods enjoyed the authority of respected tradition, but minds increasingly accustomed to question and to historicize could hardly overlook the fact that the gods had been the creation of very human poets.

Moreover, even the more skeptical had their doubts blunted by the not unreasonable conviction that all historical myths must have grown from a seed of truth. "All fables," Vives told his English readers, "have arisen out of the truth of actual events."[15] Most of a century later, Sandys is confidently maintaining that "the poets did write the truth though they writ it disguisedly."[16] And Samuel Purchas has tipped the scale of ambivalence only a little farther toward skepticism. Speaking of the "fabulous voyages" of such as Bacchus, Hercules, and Ulysses: "It is not the fable or falsehood which we seek in fabulous Antiquities, but that truth which lieth buried under poetical rubbish. For nothing but nothing can arise of nothing. Some truth therefore gave occasion to the fables."[17] Echoed and reechoed, this formula served after a fashion to bridge the gap between rational criticism and credulity. Yet with increasing difficulty. Reflecting the growing respect among scholars for solid evidence, Purchas goes on to admit that he was "weary of travelling in such loose sandy soil, where so few footprints and paths of truth are to be found."[18]

Ambivalence was not much talked about, as such—one does not proclaim ambivalence. It may well have been largely a matter of emphasis rather than of any inner dialectic. Sir Thomas Elyot, for example, appears to have taken the euhemerized gods at their face value in the thumbnail sketches of their careers he included in his dictionary, but he is careful to point out that he includes them "for the more easy understanding of poets," and not, it would seem, for purposes of historical truth.[19] For the substance of the practical, classically based education he was recommending to the English governing class, he looked to ancient history rather than to ancient mythology. Moreover, unlike the bitter debate over the British legends, classical mythology provoked neither the heat needed to melt away old ideas nor the light to distinguish fact from fiction. John Twyne, the Henrician humanist and pioneer antiquary, could be clear enough in his criticism of the legend of Britain's Trojan origin, but ambivalent about the classical myths: the tradition, for example, that Mercury had invented the arts was, he remarked, a stupid notion ("stulta opinio"), and he explained it simply as an example of how people in ancient times deified great men and credited them with superhuman accomplishments;[20] yet it does not occur to him to question whether those so deified were in fact historical personages.

Twyne's master, Vives, leaned even more toward skepticism but remained of two, albeit unequal, minds about the gods. He considered the "poets" adulterators of history and the principal cause of the confusion that made the entire period before the Olympiads an age of fable.[21] Yet he, too, had no choice but to acknowledge not only that early peoples had indeed deified great men—that was, after all, a simple fact of history—but that their gods must in reality have been persons. Among his "vetustissimi sapientes," gods and demigods brushed shoulders with men: "Mercurius, Orpheus, Hesiodus, Permenides."[22] But he found the ancient myths hard to take straight, just the same. While on a trip to the Levant, he passed up a chance to visit in Crete, the purported birthplace of Jove. The whole thing, he said, was an impious fable.[23] Compared to the biblical stories which he held to be true beyond question, the pagan myths, he said, were not histories at all, but freely concocted fables.[24] Yet he could not help believing that a core of truth remained in them.

As a historian, Ralegh was especially obliged to place the gods in historial perspective but was hampered by a similar ambivalence. He accepted the euhemerist explanation of pagan religion without question, and was able to recognize in it a historical process, though one instigated by the devil. Impressed by the apparent similarity of all primitive peoples, including the American Indians, he reached the pregnant conclusion that the elevation of mortals to the status of gods was a consistent element in the development of primitive religions. Though he devoted comparatively little space in his history to the pagan mythology, much preferring the work of "those happy hands which the Holy Ghost hath guided,"[25] he made a conscientious effort to distinguish fact from fiction and to incorporate the history supposedly contained in the fables into a chronological scheme based largely on the biblical record. He was careful, for example, to sort out the obviously fabulous element in the fables. Recognizing that the ancients tended "to call all kings Jupiter," he settled finally on the one "of whom all the Grecian fables were devised," a personage "born not long before the war of Troy." But he would not countenance all the nonsense about the deified Jupiter's "transformations into showers of gold, eagles, bulls, birds, and beasts," and did his best to link him with early monotheistic beliefs—especially, of course, with the Hebraic.[26]

Clearly there was a point beyond which Ralegh could no longer suspend disbelief. It varied a good deal, it is true, depending on the respect he had for his sources, on his own antipagan prejudice, and on the degree of affront to his common sense he experienced in reading the fables. He nurtured a bias, as much emotional as intellectual, against the entire pantheon, "that rabble of Grecian forgeries."[27] At best the pagan deities were nothing but distorted reflections of biblical personages, at worst a disreputable lot, fit role models for tyrants and courtesans.[28] He felt obliged, however, to separate the obviously incredible from what his somewhat elastic credulity allowed him to accept as credible, and from whatever could be justified as allegory. We find him weighing the story of Prometheus, for example, in a mind badly divided. Though he agreed instinctively with Cicero that Prometheus was never really bound to the Caucasus and that the fable must be taken as an allegory of divine knowledge, a turf dispute, as it were, between curious humanity and a jealous god, he had to conclude that the story of Prometheus "was not altogether fiction," and that he had actually lived about the time of Moses, as "the most approved Historians, Antiquaries, among them Eusebious and Saint Augustine, have not doubted."[29] The more the myth-history impinged on historical memory, the more Ralegh seems to have felt free to demystify it and to explain away the fabulous element. Following Herodotus, he categorized Aeneas, son of Venus, as "a bastard begotten upon some fair harlot, called for her beauty Venus," and the wolf that nursed Romulus simply as a courtesan named "Lupa, or Lupina, for the courtesans in those days were called wolves."[30]

If Ralegh reflected positions common among Elizabethans, Herbert, Lord Cherbury, rationalist and apostle of "natural" religion, spoke the unmistakable language of seventeenth-century erudition. Yet he came no nearer than Ralegh to clarifying the historical status of the gods. He passed the problem off with the confidence of a mind unaware of its own ambivalence. He referred to the "heroes" deified by the ancients—Hercules and Aesculapius, for instance, in contradistinction to the "greater gods" with whom he was apparently not prepared to deal—as "men" who "not only deserved well of their own Country but of Mankind in general" but who were shabbily treated by the Greeks and Romans, for whom there was "nothing so obscene and base, or even impious . . . [they] could not invent and relate" concerning them. Yet these stories are, Herbert maintained, "nothing but mere Fictions, which the Poets have handed us, for there is not one Writer of Prose as I know of that acknowledges any of them for the truth."[31] But it appears that the problem lies with the irresponsibility of poets who sought to outdo each other in mutual ridicule rather than with the historicity of the deified heroes. Such authors must be discarded not only because they wrote fictions but because, by mixing their fictions with "the true History of the Ancient Heroes, they have rendered the whole suspicious."[32] No doubt speaking himself from the standpoint of the more truthful prose writers, Herbert goes on to argue that those deified men were really not gods anyway, as the term is usually understood, but merely figures analogous to the "saints" of Christian tradition.[33]

Many of these men of letters, concerned with the problems of historical truth yet torn between skepticism and authority, would probably have preferred to believe if they only could. If only the "poets" had not let their imaginations run away with them, if only the early historians had not fallen prey to them and become in their turn fabulous, the seeds of truth in the fables might have germinated into plausible history. Ralegh is clearly frustrated by the equivocal evidence derived from classical sources. While conceding untenable ground, Herbert leaves the distinct impression that potentially defensible positions had been compromised by poetic tradition. And Stillingfleet blames "lack of certain [i.e., reliable] records" for the fabulous character of all Greek histories from Hesiod to the first Olympiad.[34]

The will to believe shows up still more clearly where the possibility of real documentary evidence was at least imaginable. With reference to Britain's own legendary past, doubts begin to creep in about doubt itself. Though skeptical by nature, John Selden could not help feeling that, if only more were known about the legendary past, if events had been written down instead of being left to unlettered bards—and if written then protected from the ravages of time—then sorting truth from falsehood would have been a great deal easier, and what remains hard to believe might be found to have been substantially true. In fact, however, lack of hard evidence fostered fabulous imaginings: "Too large liberty was given to feign, because of the difficulty of finding the truth."[35] John Milton found the same difficulty in dealing with Britain's prehistory: "Oftimes relations heretofore accounted fabulous have been after found to contain in them footsteps and relics of something true"—though the examples he cites, "poets of the flood, and giants little remembered," hardly justify his confidence.[36]

Such speculation as there was in Renaissance England about the place traditionally assigned to the gods in history tended to be not so much an autonomous endeavor as a by-product of public discussion—discussion, that is, of those concerns for which Renaissance writers were coming more and more to seek historical perspective. Whenever the issue involved origins, the historical imagination was bound to confront the gods, so much a part of popular prehistory they had become. Attitudes ranged from neutral to unfriendly tinged with skepticism, but were seldom overtly hostile. Invention of the arts, both mechanical and intellectual, naturally involved the deified inventors of euhemerist tradition; but, in an age of discovery, technological activity, and literary experimentation, the gods were hard put to it to maintain their relevance, let alone their historicity. On the other hand, scholarship devoted to the origins of religion and to *historia sacra* seemed as yet to leave its devotees no choice but to provide the gods with a local habitation in the scheme of history.

Not the least of the issues that inevitably involved the classical fables was the debate that took place among Elizabethan critics over the state of the English language, a debate that, given the historicizing habits of those concerned, naturally extended to the origins of poetry and of the language itself. In his *Arte of English Poesie* (published in 1589, but composed in part as much as thirty years earlier) George Puttenham offered as reasonable an explanation of euhemerism as is to be found in Elizabethan letters. It is an explanation in which tradition is balanced by a Ciceronian quality of skepticism. In the course of fulfilling the function traditionally ascribed to them as the civilizers who led mankind out of the woods and mountain fastnesses where they had lived "vagrant and dispersed like wild beasts,"[37] the earliest poets in a sense created the gods. As those who were responsible, among other things, for registering "the worthy gests of noble princes," they came to treat as gods, demigods, and heroes those men who "most resembled gods by excellency and function"—such as "Bacchus, Ceres, Perseus, Hercules, and Theseus." But this process did not necessarily guarantee historical truth. The poets have to be assessed in relation to what they had to work with, limited as they were "by the authority of their own fabulous records" (apparently written records, for he refers also to their "old written report"), which "were not from the beginning all historically true, and many of them fictitious," but (and here he cites Cicero) were "covertly applied to some moral or natural sense."[38] Puttenham further recognized that the poets could not always be taken at their word. Their account of Jupiter, for example, was a mixture of fact and fiction. His incestuous marriage with his sister could be rationalized as a custom not unusual among "Princes in the Oriental part of the world both in those days and now," and could be considered acceptable as material for "the poet historical"; but that he should "thunder and lighten and do many things very unnaturally and absurdly" was a questionable use of the poet's historical imagination.[39]

The critics who followed him and who shared his compulsion to begin at the beginning tended to confine themselves to the lesser deities who, as originators, retained a place a bit closer to the folk memory than the more remote Olympians, and to insist on an allegorical interpretation of their more fabulous feats. Amphion and Orpheus, for example, were authentic pioneers in the art of poetry, but the constantly repeated stories of Amphion building cities from the stones that came to the sound of his harp and of the wild beasts that gathered to listen to the music of Orpheus had to be taken strictly as allegories of the creative role played by poets in the dawn of civilization.[40]

The larger historical problem posed by invention of the arts might be expected to have caused more discussion than the literary debate, and to have led even more insistently to questions about the historicity of the gods, but the subject seems not to have set off a comparable debate. Passing remarks, however, indicate that the subject was nevertheless being given considerable thought. Had the arts been invented by supermen deified for their achievement, or were they divinely inspired, or were they the result of a gradual, incremental, and all but anonymous response to necessity? The question obviously struck at the very roots of the euhemerist tradition.

Most readers of Tudor England no doubt still got their notion of invention from the long-term visitor and notorious exponent of euhemerism, Polydore Vergil.[41] It remains an open question whether Polydore himself meant his *De inventoribus rerum* to be taken as historically true, or whether he was merely engaged in the scholarly task of rounding up what the respected "authors" had said about invention.[42] When dealing with the origins of a custom for which he had empirical information, he was in fact able to escape the temporal cul-de-sac of catastrophic creation, and he was able to see euhemerism itself in something like an anthropological perspective, as when he likened the Roman Catholic practice of canonizing saints to the pagan custom of deifying great men.[43] The fact remains, however, that the *De inventoribus* became, for English readers, the classic statement of the euhemerist position—especially after 1547 when a popular abridged translation appeared and reappeared for the rest of the century. English readers may have been more shocked by the mildly iconoclastic statements Polydore made in his history of England about their own national legends than excited by his pantheon of inventors, yet if they wished to find out who invented tillage, or wine making, or the alphabet, they could find a ready answer among Polydore's deities.

If, however, Polydore spoke to a century of English readers in the uncontaminated language of tradition, a new breed of scholar and intellectual-at-large, raised in the relatively realistic atmosphere of Northern humanism, was clearly gravitating toward the gradualist explanation of man's early development. Vives had already, in the earlier sixteenth century, made that theory an essential part of his philosophy of man. Invention, he insisted, could not have taken place in one sudden act—"nam nulla ars simul et inventa est et absoluta"[44]—nor were the arts either perfect or pure in their beginnings, but had evolved in response to necessity.[45]

Sir Thomas Smith came to the same conclusion with reference to the origin of writing. In his treatise on the reform of English orthography, he sought to trace language itself to its roots in the early days of the human race. Far from being an explanation, he argued, euhemerism was an impediment to understanding how language arose and diversified and how letters were invented. Such men of learning as were able to give leadership in the otherwise uncultivated conditions of the first age were indeed given divine honors, and the invention of letters was attributed to various individuals—to Thoth by the Egyptians, to Abraham by the Chaldeans, to Moses by the Jews, and so forth. But that was not how it all happened. Writing, Smith maintained, was no sudden discovery, but the result of a gradual, incremental process: "non eodem tempore, sed paulatim et per incrementa quaedam."[46]

Bacon, too, made gradualism part of what amounted, in his

writings, to a theory of cultural development and left no place at all for the gods of euhemerist tradition. As he saw it, however, innovation took place on two levels and according to contrasting principles—the one affecting the arts mechanical, the other the intellectual arts. The development of the mechanical arts had clearly been cumulative, whether by chance or by purposeful experiment, "a birth of time rather than of wit."[47] "The first deviser come shortest, and time addeth and perfecteth."[48] The intellectual arts, on the other hand, are dependent upon the wit of brilliant thinkers and are not progressive, but, like water, cannot "ascend higher than the level of the first spring-head from whence it descended."[49] (Bacon here returned very nearly to the venerable notion that man had been led out of a brutish existence in the primeval caves and forests by individuals of surpassing intelligence who inexplicably appeared among them.) Consequently, in matters of theory, of methodology if you will, advancement could not be made simply by "engrafting of new things upon old"[50] but required instead the kind of new approach he believed he was himself able to make.

The truth is that the technic gods were not so much challenged as ignored, having been rendered irrelevant by invention itself. The Big Three—the compass, firearms, and the printing press—were in fact, and to an extent that was becoming obvious to Elizabethan observers, changing their world beyond recall. Pre-Baconian Baconians of various sorts—astronomers, navigators, articulate artisans, and men of letters—were expressing by tools and pen their faith in a new and better secular life.[51] These were the men whom Samuel Daniel found ready and willing to "set their bold *Plus Ultra*"[52] well beyond the boundaries of ancient thought. In the ensuing Quarrel of the Ancients and Moderns, they and their successors abandoned the euhemerized inventors along with the ancients. Yet their quarrel remained with the ancient philosophers, not with their gods. Formal—and final—confrontation between euhemerists and gradualists had to wait until the eighteenth century. Meanwhile those who for practical purposes rejected euhemerism simply went about their business without feeling the need to engage an adversary whose stronghold was in symbol and allegory, not in history.

In ironic contrast to the decline the pagan gods appear to have suffered in their capacity as inventors was the relative prosperity they enjoyed in the context of Christian scholarship. The unprecedented interest being shown during the seventeenth century in ancient religions, though centered upon biblical scholarship, in fact did more than anything else to maintain for a while the claim of the gods to historicity of a sort. Underlying it all was the problem of chronology.[53] Despite the overwhelming authority of biblical history, the right of the pagan myths to coexist with it had achieved something like canonical status. As Higden found out in the fourteenth century, and Ralegh in the early seventeenth, any attempt to compile a universal history required the author to provide a place in his time scheme for the personages of pagan mythology. The problem of universal chronology brought out all the best—and worst—of humanist scholarship. In the light of the relatively sophisticated work of such foreign authorities as Scaliger, Vos, and Bochart, with its vastly increased knowledge of languages and cultures, and its ingenious manipulation of a philological discipline hardly yet capable of sustaining the weight of responsibility being placed upon it, chronology became an essential study also for English researchers and a favorite hobby for English gentlemen-scholars, and it continued to provide the pagan gods a place in Christian history.

The burgeoning comparative study of ancient religions, however, went much farther than chronology and came to involve the relationship perceived to exist between the history myths of all the ancient peoples. Projected largely from the standpoint of biblical scholarship, such endeavors gave the pagan gods unprecedented publicity, usually within the context of euhemerism, yet at the same time it subjected them to a critique that left them little more than shadows. By assuming the historical priority of the Hebrew language and religion, by assuming in particular that the Greek mythmakers either knew the work of Moses or preserved the essence of it in something akin to the folk memory, some of the most erudite biblical scholars of their day, in England as on the Continent, undertook to demonstrate not simply the place of the pagan gods in a Christian time frame, but the essential identity of the mythological figures with those of sacred history. As Don Cameron Allen once put it, "The search for biblical faces in the gallery of pagan gods and heroes was one of the numerous Christian obsessions of the Renaissance."[54] The unintended result was to confer upon the gods a certain reflected legitimacy, yet in the increasingly harsh light of comparative studies, it was a legitimacy that tended to fade.

The idea that the Greek deities were really reflections of, corruptions of, or in some manner borrowings from Hebrew originals underlies the thinking of Ralegh and Sandys, and after them that of the more scholarly Stillingfleet, the Puritan John Owen, to say nothing of that prolific eccentric Alexander Ross.[55] Accordingly, for example, Adam could reappear as Saturn, or perhaps Noah, in which case Neptune, Pluto, and Jupiter could be equated with Noah's sons—Japhet, Shem, and Cham. This supposed transmission and transmogrification of the mythical history in fact attained a complexity that would surely have overtaxed less sturdy wits. Certain especially erudite seventeenth-century philologists were even busy analyzing Homer as, in his way, a biblical scholar, his legends and values supposedly reflecting a Hebraic education and the substance of scriptural tradition.[56] Though the otherwise influential voice of Samuel Bochart warned that most apparent borrowings were really accidental parallels, his advice seems not to have checked the enthusiasm of the Hebraists.[57]

Merely identifying the pagan myths with Scripture did not, of course, dispose of the problem of their historicity. It no doubt reduced their importance in the scheme of history, but it left them there nonetheless. As Stillingfleet saw it, the gods lived on not only within the shadow of *historia sacra* but because of it. Although the "first ages" were "confessed to be poetical, and to have no certainty of truth in them,"[58] and the oldest Greek histories were full of fables (to Stillingfleet all but falsehoods),[59] those fables nevertheless retained traces of what Stillingfleet liked to think of as the faint but unmistakable "footsteps of Scripture-history."[60] "Memory of the Deluge," he believed, remained in the story of Deucalion's flood, and "many parcels of Noah's memory were preserved in the scattered fragments of many fables, under Saturn, Janus, Prometheus, and Bacchus." Though shadows based upon the "feigning" of poets, the gods remained, for Stillingfleet and his generation, shadows of figures who enjoyed a real, if borrowed, historicity.[61] Like Ralegh, who nourished a remote hope that, as he put it, "the rude resemblance" between "the tales of the Libyan gods and the Egyptian fables of Osiris" could one day be taken "for the crooked images of some true history,"[62] Stillingfleet could not rid his mind of the belief that some "faint and obscure resemblance of truth" clung to the fables of the poets, though so adulterated in the process of transmission that, in the absence of corroborative evidence, it had lost most of its credibility.[63] The historicity of the fables had clearly been diluted, but by no means destroyed.

At best, the comparative study of religion required its participants to accept the making of myths as a process in the history of culture. (In the next chapter we shall explore some of the ramifications of this fact.) If doing so did not dispose scholars to skepticism, it did dispose them to treat all historical mythmaking, with the still only tentatively debated exception of the Mosaic history, as an ongoing and essentially human effort, modified by the conditions inevitably affecting the transmission of culture.

The crisis of belief and understanding foreshadowed in Renaissance attitudes toward the classical history myths involved a complex interaction, in some respects a conflict, among euhemerist historism, resurgent allegorism, endemic skepticism, and a typically Renaissance compulsion to rationalize and historicize.

The difference between the euhemerist tradition and the Renaissance vogue of allegory was, to be sure, one of genre and of divergent perceptions of truth rather than conflict. By virtue of its infinite capacity for giving concrete form to abstract ideas, allegory had always commanded more attention than euhemerist speculation. Now, as freshly energized by the Neoplatonic penchant for symbolic expression, allegory bade fair rather to overwhelm euhemerist interpretation than to deny its validity. Allegory, however, was in essence ahistorical and timeless; and preoccupation with it could become, in effect, antihistorical—as when Alexander Ross insisted on finding Christian truths adumbrated allegorically throughout the fables.[64]

The tendency for allegory to dominate treatments of mythology became especially apparent during the latter half of the sixteenth century in the work of the great Continental mythographers who proceeded on the assumption, made explicit by Conti in his *Mythologiae,*[65] that the ancient poets themselves had meant their fables to be taken allegorically. If, however, those authors "forced the gods back into the matrix of allegory," as Jean Seznec maintained,[66] they did not relieve them entirely from their customary duties as historical personages. Conti, the most influential of them all, carried on the tradition of treating the myths both historically (i.e., literally) and allegorically, and, while insisting that the stories were "feigned," on occasion he lets the reader know that the person about whom the fable was feigned was indeed one who had once lived among mortals. He takes pains, for example, to establish—and in the shadow of the Inquisition piously to deplore—the unregenerate humanity of Jupiter.[67] Yet whatever core of historical truth he notes he clearly subordinates to the allegory. Ambivalence, it would seem, was built into the mythological tradition itself.

Abraham Fraunce, the interpreter of Ovid to Elizabethan readers, gave special emphasis to the "allegorical" at the expense of the "historical" by relating the possible levels of meaning that could be derived from the fables to the sophistication of the reader. "Famous exploits of renowned Heroes," he wrote, are entertaining enough to those of "rural humour"; those, however, who can go farther "than external discourse and history, shall find a moral sense . . . extolling virtue and condemning vice"; those "born of a more noble spirit, shall meet with hidden mysteries of natural, astrological or divine metaphysical philosophy."[68] Despite Fraunce's patronizing attitude, the historical sense remains clearly a part of the mythological record and of the mythographer's responsibility, and euhemerism remains capable both of conferring historical validity on the gods and of reflecting important facts of actual history. Thus Fraunce writes: "Historically, Jupiter having freed his father from thraldom took upon himself the dignity and regiment of Crete, enforcing Saturn to flee to Italy, where he was honored living and dying as a god: for such was the custom of the age, to attribute divine honour and titles unto them as gods, of whom they received any goodness."[69]

Of the other attempts at systematic mythology—those of Batman, Sandys, Bacon, and Ross—all, with the exception of Bacon, followed much the same pattern: elaborate allegory built upon the twin assumptions of initial purpose and euhemeristic biography. How significant was this residue of euhemerism in relation to the dominant allegory is, of course, impossible to tell. The gods were so ubiquitous in the culture of Renaissance England, serving an appetite for metaphor and simile so voracious, and made so familiar in emblem and impress, that to question their possible historicity would have seemed irrelevant, not to say impertinent. It has been said that, in the celebrations accompanying Elizabeth's progresses, even the pastry cooks were expert mythographers, capable of depicting the personages of Ovid's *Metamorphoses* in elaborately constructed confections;[70] and it is fair to say that neither they nor their patrons could have cared less whether the figures they depicted were truly historical. Everywhere, in literary discourse and pageantry as in manuals of mythology, the gods retained an aura of presumptive humanity, while any question as to their actual historicity was being lost in a fog of ahistorical allegory. The myth-history tended, at best, to be viewed only in the ambiguous context of what Spenser liked to call "poesie historical."[71]

Bacon provides a more complex example. He was in certain respects unique. He seems not to have cared whether the gods themselves were historical. Though he was capable of asserting that Pan was "one of the oldest gods, and long before Ulysses,"[72] he treated the gods as symbols and little more but found their symbolism of the utmost historical significance. He had come—slowly, he said—to the conclusion that "beneath no small number of the fables lay from the beginning a mystery and an allegory,"[73] and, more important, that within the allegory there lay a wisdom, since lost, but still able to be partially regained. Despite the generally secular character of his thought and his commitment to the evidence of experience as the basis for the reorganization of learning that he was proposing, Bacon could not help assessing his wisdom of the ancients in relation to the catastrophic significance of the Fall.[74] But he believed that event had a dual significance: "Man," he wrote, "by the Fall fell at the same time from his life of innocency and from his domination over creation. Both of these losses can in this life be in some part repaired; the former by religion and faith, the latter by arts and sciences.[75] It was to the realization of this latter end that Bacon hoped the timeless wisdom contained in the Greek myths might contribute.

Allegory eventually lost favor in the English intellectual community. By the early years of the eighteenth century, it was becoming ever clearer that the gods had outlived their literary usefulness, even before Samuel Johnson banished them, and the recognized value of their stories as folklore and as material for the study of primitive religion was fast replacing their philosophical value. As allegory lost favor, however, the gods enjoyed a temporary resurgence of recognition as historical personages. The neo-euhemerism of the later seventeenth and early eighteenth centuries was, in a sense, a backlash against the usurpation of the ancient myths by the allegorists. Although Thomas Blackwell, one of the most sensitive eighteenth-century interpreters of classical mythology, advised against taking the myths too literally and urged that readers pay more attention to what they meant to the ancients themselves,[76] the many readers of the Abbé Banier were being told that the gods were indeed deified mortals and hence legitimately historical.

Meanwhile, however, the gods were becoming increasingly vulnerable to rational criticism, much of it meant, oddly enough, to sustain them. It took two discrepant but not unrelated forms: first, a skeptical rationalism of the kind endemic in Renaissance England—not the skepticism, more common on the Continent, that ended by doubting the very possibility of achieving historical truth but a deep-seated distrust of explanations not compatible with reason and experience; second, and largely in reaction to the first, a compelling and ultimately self-destructive urge to rationalize in order to believe, to make credible the incredible. The former tendency should need no further illustration in this chapter, the latter may.

The urge to rationalize, to historicize, in order to make the legendary and mythical prehistory believable is more concretely exemplified in the efforts made to bend the techniques of humanist scholarship to prove the authenticity of the national legends, or in the biblical scholarship that emerged in the seventeenth century, than in any attempt to rationalize the euhemeristically interpreted myths. As we shall see in a later chapter,[77] the supporters of the legend of the Trojan origin of Britain became so entangled in a tissue of learned absurdities that they eventually defeated themselves and gave the victory by default to the proponents of a new and essentially empirical scholarship. Much the same thing was happening to the historical mythology of the Judaeo-Christian tradition, only more slowly and subtly.[78] Failure to make the Bible stories convincing as history by ingeniously contrived naturalistic arguments—efforts to locate the Garden of Eden, for example, or to explain the logistics of Noah's Ark, or to rationalize the repopulation of the world after the Flood—in the long run eroded faith in the literal historicity of Scripture and helped usher in a new criticism capable of viewing Genesis in the light of history. It was a slow process, however. The commentators whose traditionalist elaboration of Genesis had become virtually canonical retained their authority well into the seventeenth century,[79] and *historia sacra* remained sacrosanct for a good deal longer. The historical myths involved in the Greco-Roman religious traditions enjoyed, it is true, certain inherent advantages. By virtue of their extreme usefulness as adjuncts to literary expression and their comparative irrelevance as history, they were to some extent shielded from both the self-destructive urge to rationalize at all costs and from the equally destructive urge to doubt. The British legends enjoyed no such immunity. In addition to their continued usefulness as the source of literary tropes, they were still very relevant to the Englishman's sense of history. On the other hand, the pagan myths could not claim for their marvels anything like the immunity from rational criticism still claimed for the miracles reported in Scripture.

If given the opportunity, most educated Englishmen would no doubt have agreed with Conti, the orthodox mythographer, or Vives, the skeptical humanist, or Bacon, the rationalist, or Stillingfleet, the Christian apologist, or Sandys, the Ovidian translator, that a kernel of truth remained within the fabulousness of the fables.[80] The problem was how to get at it. The ancients, as usual, seemed to have shown how, though sometimes in ways that made it easier to take historical shortcuts than to face the problem squarely. Not only had Euhemerus himself reduced the gods to human proportions, but his imitator, Palaephatus, proceeding on the theory that what had once been seen could still be seen, had undertaken in his treatise *De incredibilibus* to demonstrate that a believable history lay encased in the fables that "the poets" had deliberately made fabulous in order to capture the minds of simple men.[81] Without questioning the divinity of the greater gods, he showed how it was possible to rationalize the stories of the lesser deities, demigods, and heroes, in accordance with experience. The fable of Daedalus and Icarus, incredible as it stands, thus becomes credible when it is learned that Daedalus escaped from Crete not by flying but in a fast boat, and that Icarus simply fell overboard in a storm. Or, again, clearly no bull or any other animal known to man could have borne Europa over the sea from Tyre to Crete, and anyway Jupiter could surely have found a better way of doing the job if he had really wanted to. The truth is, Palaephatus assures us, that the lady was carried off by a man named "Bull" who happened then to be fighting in the neighborhood of Tyre.[82] One may wonder which was more absurd, the fables or the rationalizations. To judge from the number of translations and editions of the *De incredibilibus,*[83] Renaissance readers must nevertheless have found it a source of considerable intellectual comfort. Well into the seventeenth century we find Sir Thomas Browne still advising his readers to rely on the rationalizations of Palaephatus as an antidote to the fabulous element that was apparently continuing to confuse their perception—and his—of the mythical prehistory.[84]

Plato's many devotees might, on the other hand, have found in *Phaedrus* a passage that would have cast the cooler light of common sense upon such efforts to rationalize the fables. Asked if he believed the story about Boreus carrying off Orithya from the banks of Ilissus, Socrates answers that if he did not already doubt the tale, as wise men do, he could rationalize it by arguing that, while Orithya was at play, a northern gust carried her over the neighboring rocks to her death. But he suggests that those who are accustomed to devising such explanations are wasting their time, adding that such efforts will in any case be never-ending: "When he has once begun, he must go on and rehabilitate centaurs and chimeras dire . . . and numberless other inconceivable and impossible monstrosities and marvels of nature. And if he is skeptical about them and would fain reduce them all to the rules of probability, this sort of crude philosophy will take up all his time."[85] But Renaissance commentators were not to be deterred. The further rationalization proceeded, the more was needed, until, as the neo-euhemerists of the early Enlightenment were to demonstrate, the effort to explain away the incredible left nothing standing but unqualified assertions of historicity based, ironically, on faith rather than reason.

Whether the gods asserted a spuriously rationalized claim to historicity or retired to the unassailable protection of allegory, in Renaissance England erosion of belief proceeded, in fact, slowly and irregularly—like a force of nature, hard for contemporaries to notice and historians to trace. Skepticism went its way, but quietly, and, except when it encountered Christian beliefs, its presence was marked more by passing remarks than by reasoned statements of principle. This should not be surprising. To Renaissance minds the supernatural was still a real presence. Even Bacon was at one point able to suggest in all seriousness a "history of marvels" as part of the reorganization of all learning that he hoped to inaugurate, a project from which "the superstitious narrations of sorceries, witchcrafts, dreams, divinations and the like, where there is an assurance and clear evidence of the fact" were not to be "altogether excluded."[86] Though he later backed away from this sort of investigation, that he proposed it at all tells something about him and the culture in which he moved.

The threshold of credulity naturally differed among his fellow Elizabethans according to the time and the individual, but there was always a point beyond which even true believers were reluctant to go. Sooner or later, those who tried to rationalize the fables were bound to come up against an insurmountable irrationality. Some of them had always seemed too monstrous to be taken literally, a fact often cited to prove that they were indeed meant to be taken allegorically. Devoted as he was to the Ovidian version of the myths he was engaged in translating, Arthur Golding found such things as Saturn devouring his children so revolting, and the goings-on between Mars and Venus so unedifying, especially for gods, as to suggest that the storytellers must have had "further things and purposes in mind."[87] Bacon felt the same way but was perhaps more put off by the absurdity of certain fables than by their immorality: without ulterior motive, he asked, who on earth could have concocted the tale about Jupiter eating up his pregnant wife and then undertaking to bear the child himself?[88] Only as allegorical figures, one would conclude, could the Olympian deities indefinitely withstand both moral censure and ridicule.

Did Renaissance England, then, really believe that the gods and heroes of classical myth and legend once lived as personages of history? Anticlimactic as it may seem, the answer must be that no categorical answer can be given. Perhaps the question itself is beside the point. To ask persons for whom mythmaking was still a living mode of thought to give a clear yes or no answer is to be, at the least, anachronistic. A society that was itself riven by contradictions might be excused for nourishing varying, even contradictory, perceptions of truth. Yet the question has to be asked if we are to understand the nature and limitations apparent in their historical sense as it reached back into the mists of utter antiquity, into that shadowy area between the natural and the supernatural, between fact and fiction—objective history and "historical poetical"—which is where, if anywhere, the gods and heroes of quasi-historical myth lived, moved, and had their peculiar being.

Any attempt to find an answer must in any case take into account the very element of ambivalence that in itself makes a categorical answer impossible. The problem, that is, becomes a matter of estimating which way, and to what extent, the scales of ambivalence have tilted. In the case of the traditional manuals of mythology, the authors were able to dodge the question of historicity by leaning toward the allegorical rather than the literal-historical interpretation—which they nevertheless insisted on rehearsing with the face-saving qualification that it was all "feigned" by "the poets." The comments made by scholars and men of letters independently, and usually in the course of some broader disquisition, reveal, on the contrary, a frame of mind in which the scales have tipped perceptibly, but in varying degrees depending on the sophistication of the author, toward the skeptical and the historical.

That they did not tilt farther was no doubt due to a variety of things, most important perhaps the fact that English intellectuals were then only beginning to explore the nature and limitations of historical truth itself, and to mediate satisfactorily between fact and fiction, history and poetry. Nor were they easily unsettled by the intrusion of the fabulous into what passed as history. Moreover, the language of mythology, protected by the inertia of custom, was only too likely to mask the stirrings of skepticism. So it is often hard to tell whether the euhemerized gods were conceived as historical figures or as symbols, archetypical and timeless. Much also depended on the context: the more incidental the reference, the more likely it was to be couched in the language of tradition, and the author thus made to appear more ambivalent or inconsistent than it was the common lot of Renaissance writers to be. Despite these qualifications, the fact remains that English comments on the quasi-historical myths tended, where possible, to rationalize and historicize. There was, to be sure, a danger in all this. The urge to rationalize and historicize too often expended itself in ultimately futile efforts to make believable the unbelievable and to treat euhemerism as proof of the historicity of the gods rather than as a custom characteristic of pagan religion.

The pseudo-history of fable could not serve indefinitely as prehistory, and by the end of the Renaissance that fact was becoming apparent to all sensitive enough to a changing intellectual climate to take notice. By then the House of Myth may seem to have been little altered since medieval times, but it was actually being saved from ultimate retirement as a "historical monument" by being put to new uses. As it declined as a center for euhemeristic studies, or even for the more traditional study of allegory, it was already promising to be what it would one day become in fact, an institution for anthropological investigation and for inquiry into the history of primitive religions. Portraits of the gods and goddesses still hung on its walls as reminders of their exploits, but that honor was due less to the stubbornly persisting euhemerism of patrons than to a rising appreciation of what the ancient deities and their fables meant to the ancients themselves, and to what they might again mean as archetypes.

3

The Age of Myth

One sign that the gods of Olympus were slipping from the confines of historical time is the tendency of those English men of letters who probed the mists of utter antiquity to ignore them in favor of mythology itself. The question accordingly becomes not so much whether, or how far, they believed in the historicity of the gods, but to what extent they were able and willing to contemplate the myths, not primarily as sources of historical fact, however veiled, but as evidence of a stage in the history of civilization, a primitive age that deified its heroes and expressed itself in poetry and fable. It was a shift rather in emphasis than in belief. Few as yet seem to have felt strongly enough about the traditional mythology to go out of their way to challenge it, and none in any systematic way. But, as noticed in the preceding chapter, there are signs of a gradual erosion of belief, a tipping of the scales of ambivalence toward the skeptical. As it lost credibility as an argument for the historicity of the gods, however, euhemerism became, for a few rare minds, all the more important as a fact in the history of society itself. Whether or not the gods were historical, their fables clearly were.

Most English authors who sought to place the mythopoeic process within the parameters of historical time usually had other purposes primarily in mind—philosophical disquisitions, literary criticism, or doctrinal polemic. But they were for that very reason able to bring to the problem a sense of history marked by a newly acute perception of period and process. It was a perception fortified during the troubled Tudor and early Stuart years by public discussion of contemporary issues which, when viewed in the perspective of history, tended to heighten awareness of the relativity of customs and beliefs to the circumstance of time and place. By the same token, the more perceptive of those who found the mythic prehistory a subject relevant to their interests came to appreciate that the ancient myths had emerged at some point in the course of man's slow climb from primitive barbarism to relative civility, and to think of them as the characteristic expression of a unique culture, one for which, in the absence of systematically compiled archaeological evidence, they served as essential documentation.

In a sense, there was little new about organizing the past in terms of stages, periods, or ages. The concept of stages was as ancient as Hesiod and as modern as Compte. But, as in the classic series from golden age to iron age in grimly descending order, the concept was meant to organize the past philosophically rather than historically. So, up to a point, was the notion of an age of myth, but what made it somewhat different was that it depended to an appreciable extent on empirical evidence and tended to be integrated into the perceived reality of universal history. Evidence for the primitive stage that the age of myth was generally supposed to represent could have been derived from study of the myths themselves in the light of the increasingly realistic scholarship that stemmed from humanism, or it could simply have become apparent when the historical imagination took up, by a process of reasoned conjecture, where "known" history left off, as in the reoriented myth of early man's efforts to pull himself out of a solitary and poor existence in primeval caves and forests.[1]

Placing the mythopoeic process within the context of historical time meant, of course, accepting the limitations inherent in any attempt to organize prehistory. Renaissance thinkers knew, as did those of classical antiquity, that anyone who tried to explore the past beyond the range of recorded history did so at his own risk. Echoing Varro, Vives once declared that everything before the Olympiads was "confused and obscure."[2] A century later, Bacon made much the same point: "The most ancient times (except what is preserved of them in scripture) are buried in oblivion and silence."[3] Yet the scholarly desire to impose some kind of order, some rational time scheme, upon the mythic past, and so to integrate it into a universal history, proved stronger than scholarly caution, or than the skepticism likewise stirring since the later Elizabethan years.

Elizabethan and early Stuart authors were better able than their predecessors to perform the relatively sophisticated feat of thinking in terms both of period and process. Medieval English commentators knew perfectly well that Greek mythology represented the peculiar expression of Greek religion, and euhemerism had provided them with a ready explanation of idolatry. Yet, with the partial exception of Reginald Pecock, they were not in the habit of viewing their mythical figures across a chasm of time, or in terms of development: idolatry remained for most of them as contemporary as heresy, and the gods as current as chivalry—thus even Pecock could in all seriousness envision the gods holding jousts on Mount Olympus.[4] Elizabethan commentators came to see the myths and the mythmakers more nearly in the perspective of time. Schooled more in public discussion, in an attempt to call in the past to redress the balance of the present, than in formal historiography, they were becoming better able to recognize whatever was distinctive about past ages and to appreciate the processes of change. More immediately, they were able to call upon a newly energetic scholarship devoted to the study of chronology. Following in the wake of Continental scholarship, especially that of Scaliger, who set a new standard for chronological study in his *De emendatione temporum* (1583), a few English students of chronology undertook to place the events and personages of pagan mythology into temporal relationship with the biblical tradition, to carry the whole story back to the Creation, and to present it all in a single integrated scheme without suspicious gaps or breaks in the orderly sequence of generations.[5]

Much as this attention to chronology may have done to give the myth-history a place in the universal time scheme, it did little to establish whether, or when, there had ever been a time peculiarly marked by expression in myth and poetry. What led Protestant England to the study of chronology was, after all, not so much a disinterested desire to clarify the perspective of history as a compulsion to bring universal history into accord with the biblical narrative. Indeed, to the dedicated Puritan, to William Harrison, for example, who devoted much of his energies and not inconsiderable learning to the subject, chronology was dominated by the story of God's covenant with man—to history, that is, as prophecy, complete with the subtly antihistorical device of prefiguration.[6]

Synchronizing sacred and pagan histories was, of course, by no means easy. Unless, like Ludowick Lloyd, the chronologer was able to discount all pagan sources on the ground that they had not consulted Hebrew histories, and so, in effect, to dodge the problem,[7] or, like Stillingfleet among a more sophisticated generation of critics, to identify the characters of pagan mythology with those of sacred history, the best that England's amateur chronologers could do was simply to list the two in parallel columns according to their supposed dates. By the mid-seventeenth century, however, the problem of an age of myth had taken on a life of its own not necessarily dependent upon the insights of chronologers, professional or amateur. Here, as was then so often the case, historical insights tended to be the by-product of discussions of things other than history per se—in comments on Ovid, for example, or debates concerning the nature of poetry, or controversies over biblical interpretation.

In their effort to identify an age of myth as a time in the evolution of civilization, and as a concept independent of *historia sacra,* certain thinkers were able to draw upon the confessionally neutral resources of their classical heritage. This was especially true in the case of Varro, whom the Renaissance knew largely by way of Augustine. Varro had long been accepted as an authority on the mythical past, but in the historicizing atmosphere of the Renaissance his dicta regained a certain freshness. Whatever opinion Varro may have had about the overall direction of history, he apparently did undertake to analyze his own mythological heritage in periodic terms. He was known to have identified three successive states: first, the unknown time, from Chaos to the deluge of Ogyges, the time of the gods; second, the fabulous period that lasted until the Olympiads, the time of the heroes and demigods (Scaliger had preferred to call it "heroic" rather than "fabulous"); and third, the "historical," dating from the Olympiads, the time covered by recorded history.[8]

The importance of the Olympiads as a boundary line of sorts separating the age of myth from the "historical" had been recognized in the early sixteenth century by Vives. Although he did not use Varro's tripartite time scheme, he cited him in support of his own thesis that, since the time prior to the first Olympiad was one about which it was impossible to know anything certain, full poetic license would have to be given to those poets whose fables amounted to a bogus history, more "lies" than truth.[9] At one point, he identified this pre-Olympian age with a primitive stage in the development of mankind, a time of crudeness and credulity.[10]

Some Elizabethan commentators were pleased to adopt Varro's

dictum as it stood. Others adapted it to suit their own preconceptions. Camden took it straight from Varro and found it useful in his effort to undermine the authenticity of Geoffrey's account of British origins: what he wrote about belonged not to the "historical" period but to the "fabulous."[11] No doubt reflecting Scaliger's influence, Selden made the distinction between a "primitive" and a "heroic" age, between "true history" and what "the philosophers call myth," an essential part of his historical philosophy.[12] George Sandys undertook to accommodate the tradition of Varro with that of *historia sacra*.[13] Assuming that the Bible provided the only true guide to ancient history, he found that "the almost worn-out steps of Antiquity" led back to the period from Creation to Noah's flood, the time "which the Ethnics called obscure." Then, in due course, followed the "heroical" and the "fabulous," so-called because "these stories conveyed traditions in loose and broken Fragments, [which] were by the Poets interwoven with instructing Mythology, . . . and most obscurely and perplexedly delivered by all but the supernaturally inspired Moses." In his *De re poetica* (1573), Richard Wills apparently found Varro's dictum capable of being adapted also to the less closely related history of ancient poetry: first, the primitive and uncultivated period ("priscum, rude, et incultum"), devoid of record, "unless Apollo be recognized as the foremost representative"; second, the time during which pagan mythology ("priscum Ethnica theologia et mysteria") emerged, the time of "Orpheus, Musaeus, Linus, and Olympus"; and, finally, the period during which the ancient fables were relayed to later generations by Homer and Hesiod.

Contemporary scholarship did much to lend meaning to the perception of an age of myth. In a characteristic effort to set the problem in historical perspective, such literary critics as Wills found the early history of poetry intimately associated with that of mythology. As noticed in the preceding chapter, George Puttenham in particular saw that, in the process of fulfilling their function as general-purpose intellectuals and, more particularly, as praisers of famous men, the earliest poets had naturally become euhemerizers, and to that extent had created the corpus of ancient fable and, in a sense, the gods themselves. It was biblical scholarship, however, that did most to cast light upon the age of myth, if only obliquely. The reader may recall that, as part of a concerted effort to explore the ancient cultures, and especially to examine the relationship between the Hebrew tradition and that of pagan antiquity, scholars found themselves engaged in comparative studies in which their philological learning had considerably outrun their knowledge of mankind.[14]

The idea that the Greek myths, in particular, had somehow evolved from an original Hebrew tradition embodied in Scripture had become generally accepted theory; and the pagan gods had achieved quasi-historical status as a result, if only by reflection from their Hebrew original. The idea permitted scholars to study the migration of the gods as typical of a certain stage in the history of civilization, a period marked by internal process and change as much as by generally applicable characteristics.

It was in this light that Ralegh, for one, chose to view the Greek history myths. The idea that the gods represented corruptions of Hebrew originals proved as useful to him as to the more highly specialized of his contemporaries, but he chose to interpret the process not simply as one of acculturation, but of conscious conspiracy. The Greeks, he maintained, had really stolen their gods. They had adapted the Word of God to their liking and then passed it off as their own: "By fabulous inventions, and by breaking into parts the stories of Creation, and by delivering it over in a mystical sense, wrapping it up mixed with other their own trumpery, [they] have sought to obscure the truth thereof; and have hoped that after ages . . . might receive these intermixed discourses of God and nature for the inventions of poets and philosophers, and not as anything borrowed or stolen out of the book of God."[15] This is how Adam, for example, became the prototype of Saturn, and Cain that of Jupiter, how legends such as those of Hercules were adapted from Scripture, and how the pagan gods came to personify universal virtues and vices. The fables were, in short, an aberration, a deviation from the main line of biblical history. Though the Greeks adopted them as their own, they found them originally as a result of something like an archaeological accident. They took the fables from "relics of ancient records" that the Egyptians and others had found inscribed "on stones and metal" after the Flood. It was on the basis of these fragments that, according to "Augustine out of Varro," "Saturns, Vulcans and Mercuries" of Greek tradition were invented "by imitation."[16]

Certain of Ralegh's successors, less bound than he by tradition and more versed in the new comparative scholarship taking shape during the first half of the seventeenth century, were able to bring to this same problem a more sophisticated conception of historical process. The Puritan divine, John Owen, carried on the search for the Christian origins of pagan mythology on the familiar assumption that the Greeks got their myth-history from the Hebrew, transmitted by such other Semitic peoples as the Phoenicians.[17] But it was Edward Stillingfleet who developed a similar line of thought most effectively for English readers.

To Stillingfleet's rational and historically conditioned mind, understanding the process by which biblical tradition reappeared in corrupted form in pagan myths was a prerequisite to establishing the truth of what he chose to call "Scripture-history." He was following, he said in his *Origines Sacrae* (1663), the method Thales used in estimating the height of the pyramids by means of the length of their shadows: "So shall we the height and antiquity of truth from the extent of the fabulous corruption of it."[18] The task involved a critical, if highly tendentious analysis of the age of myth, and in significant depth.[19] By comparing the Greek myths—in his mind the most corrupting as well as the most corrupted—with the more venerable ones of the Phoenicians, Egyptians, and Chaldeans (and, of course, the Hebrews, considered the most "primitive" of all) and by leaning heavily on recent Continental scholarship, especially that of the Netherlanders Vos and Bochart, he was able to explain the age of myth, or, as he preferred to call it, "the age of poetry," in terms of the transmission and evolution of ideas. Stillingfleet saw Greek mythology as at once unique and derivative, and the age in which it arose and flourished both a recognizable period and one marked by a process of degeneration.

He traced that process, moreover, to certain underlying causes. He found a taproot of the problem in "the gradual decay of knowledge and increase of Barbarism in the world, occasioned by the want of certain [i.e., reliable] Records," as a result of which "there must needs follow a sudden and strange alteration of the memory of former times." (Why the decay of knowledge was "gradual" but the alteration of memory "sudden" need not detain us: consistency was not Stillingfleet's strongest suit.) The problem had then become exacerbated by the confusion of languages at Babel, by the rise of idolatry, and by the pagan custom of deifying mortal men.[20]

But the efficient cause he found in the poets themselves, considered as mythmakers, and in the process by which they elaborated and transmitted their fabulous history.[21] While agreeing that the earliest poets had indeed made it possible for the Greeks to "creep out of barbarism," he accused them of so corrupting their historical tradition with fabulous elements that the historians who came after them were unable to retrieve the truth and had to confess their essential ignorance of those earliest times. Beginning "about the time of Orpheus," and "increasing still in the times of Homer and Hesiod," poets made that "poetic age" truly an age of myth. Following Strabo's disenchanted interpretation, Stillingfleet pictured the poets not merely as instructors but as pragmatists ready to serve the ends of rulers by using fables "the better to awe the silly multitude, and so bring them into better order," a program that included the perverse mythology inherent in idolatry.

Self-serving and cynical as these poets-as-propagandists may have seemed, Stillingfleet came to see that the process of "alteration" for which they were responsible was the result of long-range and impersonal tendencies within ancient culture. The earliest Greek poets, he said, tended to assume that everything conveyed to them by the ancient tradition had been part of their own history.[22] They attributed "what was done by the great Ancestors of mankind to persons of their own nation." So, for example, Jupiter was made to play for them the part of Jehovah, and Deucalion and his flood the part of Noah and his.[23] They also substituted for names in the ancient tradition "those of like importance in their own language."[24] Or they conflated the stories of several persons and attributed them to one who was chief among them. Thus the stories of "Mars, Mercury, Minerva, Juno, Bacchus, and Hercules" became "a collection of the actions done by a multitude of persons"; and most Greek kings before the Trojan Wars were called "Joves."[25] Stillingfleet realized, too, that the poets had responded to circumstances inherent in the very language they used. They tended to take the figurative idioms of their "oriental" sources literally, as when the notion of Bacchus being born of Jupiter's thigh stemmed from the Hebraism "wherein coming out of the thigh is a phrase of ordinary procreation."[26] Or, again, when their sources were ambiguous, they tended to take the more fabulous sense instead of the "plain and obvious." The fable of the Golden Fleece accordingly became "nothing else but the robbing the treasury of the King of Colchis," the confusion having arisen because the same Syriac word meant both "fleece" and "treasury."[27]

Stillingfleet's analysis reflected the limitations of contemporary scholarship as well as its insights. It was characterized by an uneven blend of tradition and criticism, credulity and common sense. It reflected, above all, the assumption of inevitable corruption that so permeated attitudes toward the history of civilization on the eve of the Quarrel of the Ancients and Moderns, an assumption against which Francis Bacon and George Hakewill, each in his own way, strove.[28] But it also reflected the best biblical scholarship of the late Renaissance, with all its prodigious philological learning—to say nothing of its residual credulity and the runaway ingenuity that then all too often passed for scholarship. Stillingfleet's sensitivity to both period and process reveals something of the historical relativism that, in England, had been fostered by the use of history in public discussion more than by the writing of it.[29] His biblical scholarship shares the commonsense rationalism of his fellow latitudinarians,[30] a rationalism he believed to be as applicable to the various pagan religions of antiquity as to the "true" religion. And his analysis of the process by which the ancient myths were transferred from one culture to another proves the leavening influence of comparative studies.

In Bacon's theories of myth and history the concept of an age peculiarly given to expression in myth and symbol received the fullest treatment it was to get in England for another century. There this concept became not only explicit but virtually autonomous, based on the study of man rather than on either the Varro tradition or that erudite mixture of fable and sacred history that had energized, and also limited, Stillingfleet's sense of history. The idea of stages gave structure and meaning to Bacon's own sense of history, more especially to his perception of cultural history. He had a clear enough perception that the earliest age about which it was possible to know anything was indeed an age of myth.

"To the silence of the earliest times," Bacon wrote, "succeeded the fables of the poets: to the fables the written records which have come down to us."[31] He was too aware, however, of the relation of thought and expression to the changing circumstances of time and place to see that age of the poets as uniform. Mythmaking itself had taken place irregularly: those who drew "the veil, as it were, of fables" that separated "the hidden depth of antiquity and the days of tradition and evidence that followed" were "men who had lived in different ages and had different ends, some being more modern, some more ancient."[32] But in one way or another these myth-makers and the society they served had in common a peculiarly primitive mentality.

It is this idea of a primitive mentality that was to prove the most enlightening and lasting element of all the speculation then being made about an age of myth. Bacon found it only natural that a prelogical and preliterate age of fantasy should have preceded the age of abstract reason. Even before the days of Homer and Hesiod, ancient poets had, he said, shaped fables to the capacity of minds still "rude and impatient of all subtlties that did not address themselves to the sense"—minds much like those especially prone to Bacon's "idols of the tribe."[33] Their outlook unobscured by abstractions, these childlike folk needed to see things in terms of similitudes and parables, and in the concrete images ultimately exemplified by the hieroglyphics of the Egyptians.[34]

Few aspects of the knowledge then becoming available about earlier cultures did more to lend apparent substance to the perception of a primitive mentality as a characteristic of an age of myth than hieroglyphic art—or to provide concrete evidence for the prerational, preliterate culture Bacon had in mind. Hieroglyphics had been the source of considerable scholarly interest ever since the publication of the *Hieroglyphics of Horapallo* early in the sixteenth century.[35] The subject naturally caught the fancy of Renaissance Neoplatonists who liked to think of hieroglyphics as an esoteric system of sacred symbols; but, by the close of the century, and in the more rationalistic atmosphere of the century following, the art began to appear more as evidence of a primitive mentality than of an esoteric system.[36] At the height of the controversy over the "British History," Sir John Price argued that the bards who memorialized the heroes of England's own antiquity were simply doing for them the same kind of service as the ancients who preserved the memory of their gods in hieroglyphic symbols.[37] Stillingfleet found symbolic expression, as codified by the Egyptians and transmitted to the Greeks as a habit of thought, to be the source of the obscurity and ambiguity that made their fables bad history.[38] Bacon had been still more forthright. Hieroglyphics, together with the parabolic fables, had been invented, he claimed, not to hide a secret wisdom from the vulgar but because "it was then of necessity to express any point of reason which was more sharp or subtle than the vulgar in that manner, because men in those times wanted both variety of example and subtilty of conceit."[39] Moreover, Bacon took pains to identify hieroglyphics with both the preliterate and prerational character of an age devoted to myth: "As hieroglyphics came before letters, so parables came before arguments."[40]

Some years earlier, Samuel Daniel had associated the hieroglyphic art still more specifically with childhood—not only that of a preliterate, prerational culture, but of childhood universally.[41] Like Bacon, he associated the art with emblems and impresses, but he traced the Elizabethan vogue for such devices to the tendency of children everywhere to draw pictures. Hieroglyphics thus resulted from "a natural disposition," evident "even from the beginning when the world was but new," which first "inclined nations" to convey their thought veiled under the form of "beasts, plants, trees, celestial figures, and the like." Universal it may have been, but, as Daniel recognized, this tendency achieved its historical manifestation in the hieroglyphic art of the Egyptians, which, at its best, represented real progress over "rude antiquity," though obviously not over writing. The implication that arises from this argument is that early cultures differed from later ones not in the essentials of human nature but as childhood differs from maturity.

Ever since Augustine,[42] this analogy between the life history of the race and that of the individual had been commonly taken for historical reality. In the present context, this idea that primitive peoples represented the childhood of mankind becomes pertinent to that of an age peculiarly marked by the making of myths. The idea did not lend itself to idealizing such an age. Contrary to visions of a lost paradise, or an age of gold, or to any worship of antiquity as such, it tended to patronize the primitive mentality. Christian humanists had repeatedly asserted that God had spoken to the Jews "as to children,"[43] and, from his more secular standpoint, Bacon reminded admirers of the ancients that their own age was the real antiquity, and that the antiquity they revered really represented the youth of the world: "antiquitas saeculi juventus mundi."[44]

Baconians, however, did not need to go to ancient example for evidence of a primitive mentality: they had contemporary evidence in the increasing flow of news from the New World. The American

Indians exemplified a childhood no less real for being historically retarded.[45] By assuming the uniformity of human nature, it was easy enough to relate the Indians directly to an age of myth. With some acuity, Richard Eden, for example, noticed, in the course of his translation of Peter Martyr's *Decades of the Newe Worlde,* that the origin myths nourished by the Indians were "fables much like Ovid his transformations."[46] And Vives found the Indians similar to the Greeks at the time of their mythmaking, if only because the fables of the one and the religious imaginings of the other arose alike "ex cruditate et credulitate."[47] Assessments of the distant past on the basis of perceived similarities with contemporary savagery became, in fact, habitual during the seventeenth century, though they were too often made with little attention to the differences that should have modified such perceptions.[48]

Persuasive as it was, and seemingly in accord with experience, the notion of a primitive mentality ran counter to the widespread and apparently attractive idea that the ancient fables contained, veiled in allegory, a mysterious wisdom—pristine, yet good for all times.[49] Though apparently incompatible, these two ways of looking at the age of myth could actually coexist peaceably enough in a culture still as receptive to intimations of a prelapsarian perfection, presumed to have lingered in the minds of the mythmakers, as it was to the perception of man's progress from childhood to maturity. But it was coexistence bought at the price of ambiguity—the idea of an age of myth had to be flexible enough to fit the vision of an original and universal wisdom as well as that of a primitive and childlike mentality. As a matter of fact, thanks to the resulting ambiguity, the two visions were not usually considered mutually exclusive. The pristine wisdom of the initial mythmakers was presumably the same wisdom that, according to inveterate tradition, permitted the poets of the first age to lead primitive, quasi-feral man from the primeval caves and forests to some semblance of civility. How these poets-as-wisemen emerged from among barbarians, however, and how they were able to retain those intimations of a lost perfection that was the heritage of the original makers of the fables, and what happened to that heritage in the process of transmission remained unanswered questions. In any case, supporters of the Moderns in their emerging quarrel with the Ancients were likely to find it hard to support their position and still envision the age of myth as one illuminated by a mysteriously revealed wisdom.[50]

Yet this is precisely what Bacon undertook to do. Ironically, it was Bacon, the prophet of a new wisdom and of a new method "not fetched out of the darkness of antiquity,"[51] the historian happy to identify the age of myth with the childhood of the race, who, alone among his English contemporaries, gave sustained thought to the arcane wisdom of the ancients.

In a spirit of typically Elizabethan pragmatism, Bacon was able to convince himself that the ancient fables reflected a wisdom largely lost since the Fall, but capable of being in substantial part regained through the very reorganization of learning he was himself proposing.[52] He had come, he said, slowly and after much thought, to the conclusion that beneath the fables of the ancient poets there lay "an allegory,"[53] and he undertook, in his treatise *De Sapientia Veterum,* to review the corpus of Greek mythology in an effort to find in it a meaning relevant to contemporary concerns, those especially of natural philosophy; if, in the process, he interpreted some of the fables in developmental terms, as when he found in that of Prometheus a suggestion of man's potential for cultural growth,[54] it simply goes to show how flexible certain of Bacon's historical concepts really were, and in this instance it tends to redeem his perception of early human society from utter paradox.

Bacon himself seems to have recognized how tenuous such interpretations of early culture must always be. "It may be," he wrote, with less confidence than was his wont, "that my reverence for primitive times may have carried me too far," yet he found "the frame and texture of the fables" to conform so closely to "the thing signified" as to indicate that the original mythmakers meant to convey a message, whether or not they had set out to "disguise and veil the meaning" or "to clear and throw light upon it."[55] And he stretched the essentially traditional, basically allegorical methods of interpretation as far as they would go in order to tap this vein of original wisdom.

What best reveals Bacon's perception of an age of myth, however, is not his handling of the myths themselves, but his concern with the mythmakers and with mythmaking. In this respect the introduction to the *De Sapientia* becomes more revealing than the body of the text—which in any case is far from original.[56] There Bacon presents the problem of myth, not in the static and archetypical terms of an original wisdom, but in those of process, of how the myths were made. Did the allegory arise as an interpretive reading of an existing fable, or did the message precede the fable and give rise to it? After much thought Bacon had come finally to the latter conclusion. He recognized that the transmission of the fables was a long process and that an age of myth had to be identified in the context of movement and change. He understood the importance of oral tradition. He knew that the fables were not invented by those who first gave them their classic expression—"Homer, Hesiod and the rest"—but that in their varying forms they had come down to succeeding ages "as sacred relics and light airs breathing out of better times, that were caught from the traditions of more ancient times and so received into the flutes and trumpets of the Greeks."[57]

Much as Bacon venerated the wisdom he believed veiled under the allegory of the fables, he was prepared to treat them and their makers in terms of historical criticism. Did the mythmakers really know what they were doing, he asked, or were they merely lucky to have chanced upon material so likely to inspire contemplation? Either way, he noted cannily, he himself could hardly lose by studying their legacy, since by doing so he would be "throwing light either upon nature or upon antiquity itself." This statement suggests that Bacon was quite aware of the two possible and potentially contradictory approaches to the age of myth. What is more, he may well have seen them as complementary rather than contradictory at all. Whereas the approach via "nature," the universal and immutable essence of which the ancients spoke, in their wisdom or innocence, was the legitimate object of philosophical speculation, the approach via "antiquity" was the legitimate object of historical investigation—of inquiry, that is, into that which is subject to change and is relative to time and place.

The problem the ancient fables posed for Renaissance thinkers was not so much one of belief or unbelief—the myth-history could not be exorcised in any case by the techniques as yet available, even if those concerned had been of a mind to do so—but rather one of history itself. Though enhanced to the point of obvious absurdity by the poetic imagination, the corpus of historical mythology constituted a record that, for lack of any but the most elementary archaeological or anthropological tools, could not be ignored by anyone interested in the "first age." But a few scholars were coming to see that its value as history derived less from the stories it contained than from its very existence. The more skepticism ate away the credibility of the fables, the greater was the tendency to examine them collectively as the expression of an age, and the more attention the age attracted, the more it came to be seen as a stage—or better still, a stage composed of stages—in the evolution of human culture. As a result, discussion of this perceived age of myth became, in a small but nonetheless significant way, a seminal factor in the maturing process then taking place in the more general area of historical thought.

4

A Secular Alternative

Like those pre-Socratic philosophers who turned from mythological explanations to speculation based on natural and evolutionary assumptions, a significant number of England's intellectuals found their inherited mythologies inadequate as explanations of man's earliest condition and sought one more congruent with reason and experience. The inherited myths, it is true, remained in good enough shape: whatever decline they ultimately suffered was by no means as yet apparent to the casual observer. And if the pagan myths may have lost credibility as history, those preserved in the biblical tradition still flourished. Genesis, as expanded and expounded by a succession of commentators, in fact constituted a source of authority so monumental as to be neither easily ignored nor safely contested, one indeed still taken largely for granted. Neither the classical nor the biblical tradition, however, was likely entirely to satisfy those minds who were brought up in the civic-oriented tradition of English humanism, who were interested in placing the problems of their own society in historical perspective, and who expected such a perspective to extend logically to the beginning of time. Both traditions depended for the most part on legends of deeds done by persons, be they patriarchs or euhemerized gods and heroes, but told little about man's collective life or about the evolution of society itself. Although they would not have expressed themselves in quite those terms, what Renaissance minds needed was a new myth, one that would do the service of any good historical myth by carrying the imagination beyond the point where empirical evidence leaves off yet remaining in accord with reason and experience, an essentially secular myth, uncommitted to the traditions of pagan theology, and only indirectly committed to *historia sacra*.

What Renaissance thinkers came up with was not, however, a new myth at all but another old one revived and redirected to suit their needs. Mostly either humanists or of humanistic background, they naturally found this myth in their revered classical authors—not the "poets" who sang of the gods, but those authors who like themselves had sought perspective in an imaginative reconstruction of man's earliest state. They could have found it in any number of places—probably in Lucretius, Vitruvius, Diodorus Siculus, or Cicero, or perhaps in Aristotle himself—the exact source of so ubiquitous an idea is immaterial.[1] It was, after all, an idea that could have occurred to anyone, at any time, who was able and willing to contemplate, without prejudice, the fact of man's progressive control of his environment. It had occasionally obtruded on the thought of medieval observers, but their eyes were generally turned elsewhere. In Tudor England, with its reoriented classical learning and its emerging sensitivity to the social and cultural past, the time was right. According to this tradition—for the sake of brevity let us simply refer to it as "the cave myth"—people at first lived a solitary and exiguous existence in caves and forests, not unlike brute beasts, but gradually, and in response to necessity, managed to achieve a state of comparative civility.

This pregnant speculation provided Renaissance minds, as it had those of classical antiquity, with not only an implied perspective but one that seemed validated by experience, both as recorded in history and as derived from observation of contemporary barbarism. In the religiously charged atmosphere of sixteenth- and early seventeenth-century England, it served the much-needed purpose of a confessionally neutral myth of origin. It also came to bear implications concerning the evolution of society that reached well beyond the specific problem of origins, and, as such, it becomes, for the modern historian, the key to an easily underrated aspect of Renaissance historical consciousness.

In the following pages we shall first examine the nature of the cave myth itself and then explore those of its implications that may help explain the sense of history emerging in Renaissance England.

Although the cave myth was to prove useful as a point of departure for any historically oriented argument, it in fact appealed initially, and with continued meaning, to those Tudor humanist-publicists who sought to place their comment on the issues of the day in the perspective of human history—Thomas Starkey and Sir Thomas Smith, for example, on the "very and true commonweal of this realm of England," or Sir Thomas Elyot on the education of the aristocracy, or John Twyne on the national origins, or George Puttenham and Sir Thomas Wilson on the state of poetry and rhetoric, or Richard Hooker on the "laws of ecclesiastical polity"—or, among the foreign authors most influential in England, Erasmus on war, and Vives and LeRoy on the course of civilization itself. The learning of Tudor humanists had long since become more an applied learning than one preoccupied with its own perfection. Not surprisingly, they found in early man's struggle in a rigorous environment to realize the potentialities inherent in his nature a metaphor for their own efforts in the public interest. The newly acute sense of history that marked their work had already brought the documentable past into sharper focus and was ready to pursue the undocumentable as far as the historical imagination could go and still stay within hailing distance of reason and experience. But it was public discussion rather than the demands of scholarly argument, certainly more than any academic concern with mythology as such, that sent these articulate citizens back to speculative beginnings.

To the substance of such discussions the cave myth was more often than not incidental, a point of departure and little more, and expressed in *obiter dicta* more frequently than in extended disquisition. Yet that fact can be misleading. The intellectuals of Tudor and Stuart England were not only accustomed to following the lead of history as far as it would go into the outer reaches of antiquity, but were equally ready to follow the deductive logic inherent in the process back down again to their own day. Though obviously the result rather of philosophical necessity than empirical investigation, a response to the need then commonly felt for historical understanding and psychological assurance, the cave myth became in fact a characteristic and seminal element in the mind-set of these authors.

Specific examples of the use made of the cave myth by English authors, and by foreign writers especially available to them, are too numerous to recite and tend in any case to be repetitious.[2] Thomas Starkey's version, though more opulently stated than most, may be considered roughly paradigmatic. In his *Dialogue between Pole and Lupset,*[3] his interlocutors discuss the nature of a true commonwealth and how England might be made into one. They assume that any solution to that problem must take into account the nature of man and the origins of his society. In an effort to place the problem in a historical-philosophical perspective, Pole makes a statement that, for the purposes of this study, deserves extended quotation:

A time there was, Master Lupset, as we find in stories many and diverse, when man, without city or town, law or religion, wandered abroad in the wild fields and woods none other wise than you see now brute beasts to do. At the which time he was led and drawn without reason and rule by frail fantasy and unruled affects, and so long continued and many years till at the last certain men of great wit and policy with perfect eloquence and high philosophy, considering the excellent nature and dignity of man, and perceiving right well that he was born and of nature brought forth to higher perfection than he applied himself unto, began to persuade the rest of the people to forsake that rudeness and uncomely life and so to follow some order and civility, and first of all to build them certain cities and towns, whereto they might assemble to their common aid, succor and commodity, avoiding the danger and peril of the wild beasts, by whom they were oft before devoured and destroyed, then after they devised certain ordinance and laws, whereby they might be somewhat induced to follow a life convenient to their nature and dignity. These laws and ordinance at the first beginning also were unperfect and somewhat rude according to the time and nature of the people, for it was not possible suddenly, by exact law and policy to bring such a rude multitude to perfect civility, but ever as the people by process of time in virtue increased, so perfect laws by politic men were devised, and thus in long time by perfect eloquence and high philosophy men were brought, by little and little, from the rude life in fields and woods to this civility which you now see established and set in well ruled cities and towns.[4]

This account reads like a thumbnail epic, and its outlines seem clear. Man worked his way from a quasi-feral existence to one of comparative civility in response to the exigencies of his natural environment and in accord with the potentiality inherent in his "excellent nature." But it leaves the process clouded in ambiguity. Man's rise has been indeed slow and gradual, "by little and little," but it has also been achieved not by way of the incremental contributions of numberless individuals, but by the presumable giant steps taken by culture heroes, those men of "great wit and policy" who were capable of "perfect eloquence and high philosophy."[5]

How persons of this sort arose from among the rude denizens of a primeval wilderness is left unexplained—as it was in most versions of the myth.

Man's story is clearly one of development and its outlook optimistic, even allowing for the frailty likewise inherent in his nature. It is also radically environmental. Taking his epistemology, as he said, from Aristotle, Starkey states that "the mind of man first of itself is as a clean and pure table, where is no thing printed or carved, but of itself apt and indifferent to receive all manner of pictures and image."[6] But, as Locke was to find with his own version of the tabula rasa, it is not easy to follow this apparently uncompromising position to its logical conclusion, especially when, like those of most political thinkers of early modern England, one's mind is divided between the presumed absolutes of nature's law and the perceived relativity of human efforts to the circumstances of time and place.[7] Starkey assumed that the mind of man in fact retained the inborn traits of universal humanity. The perfection inherent in his nature "standeth in reason and virtue, by which he both knoweth that which is truth and good and hath will stable and constant purpose to follow the same."[8] Qualified as his environmentalism may logically have been, it nevertheless held out for Starkey not only the possibility of reform but a plausible explanation of man's prehistory.

Although the classical myth of the caves applied strictly to man's earliest existence, as applied in Renaissance thought it acquired a certain degree of flexibility. The notion of a "first age" differed according to whether the author had in mind the very beginning of human society, either as pictured in the classical myth itself or as beginning with the Fall, or whether he dated his speculative anthropology from that second Fall precipitated by the Flood. And his orientation in this respect, in turn, depended on how willing he was to follow the classical myth more or less as given, thus escaping the restrictions imposed by the scriptural time scheme. As a matter of fact, it is not always easy to tell in which context a given author was thinking. Generally speaking, however, the more realistic the vision and the more specifically related to an interpretation of contemporary society, the more likely it was to be postdiluvian. Certainly the Flood constituted a catastrophic event in human history that could then neither be denied, despite efforts to rationalize it, nor ignored. It tended to be looked upon as in reality a new beginning, and the human condition in the postdiluvian world tended accordingly to be interpreted in terms of a primitive savagery quite in accord with the cave myth.

The vision of primitive savagery thus evoked suggested to anyone with enough sense of historical relativism to appreciate its meaning that all peoples had lived in this primitive state until history caught up with them. As an already developed civilization spread, it encountered peoples who lived much as those in the "first age." According to Ralegh, for example, this was the case when civilizers of the kind mentioned by Starkey came into Europe and, among other things, taught the native peoples, who had hitherto lived in the open on herbs and roots, to make cottages and to make bread from acorns. This age, "the same together with Moses," was also when Prometheus flourished. And Ralegh took the wide open opportunity to twit the peoples of his own day: "Judge how poor and wretched these times were, and how falsely nations have vaunted that their antiquities accompanied not only with civil learning, but with all kinds of knowledge"[9]—a lesson for those Englishmen who liked to claim immemorial antiquity for English law and to find learning alive in early Britain.[10]

We shall have to return to this perception of a universal primitivism at a later point, but it is worth mentioning here how English antiquarians were eventually able to see their own ancestors, the ancient Britons, in this same context, and how the aborigines of the New World came increasingly to serve as an especially telling example of original savagery, despite the lateness of their appearance on the historical stage. The geographer Nathanael Carpenter placed the early Europeans in the specific context of both the cave myth and New World savagery: "It is revealed by the ancients, as well of the Germans, as of our own nation, that they lived almost in the condition of wild beasts in woods and deserts, feeding like swine on herbs and roots, without law or discipline . . . little different from the present Americans, not yet reduced to civility."[11]

It is time now to examine more closely the historical-anthropological vision represented by the cave myth and, by tracing its several implications, to see how it both reflects and affects a temporal mind-set that was significantly characteristic of English thought in the Renaissance years.

Starkey himself failed to develop the cave myth further than was necessary in order to lend perspective to his analysis of a true commonwealth. He made only the briefest of conventional statements about the civilizing process. Few Tudor publicists, it is true, did much better, or as well. Most merely made the point that primeval man lived a deprived life and then, assuming without further question the developmental implications of the idea, proceeded quickly to whatever was otherwise on their mind. There are, however, notable exceptions. Sir Thomas Smith, like Bodin whose theory of the state he in fact foreshadowed, sought to ground his version in an imagined prehistory.[12] Richard Hooker interlaced the opening chapter of his magisterial *Laws of Ecclesiastical Polity* with subtle insights into primitive thought and what it implied about the evolution of society.[13] Though one of the few Elizabethans who undertook to contemplate the course of civilization without specific reference to the cave myth, Bacon made a characteristically idiosyncratic effort to penetrate the primitive mentality.[14] In addition, English readers could count on several foreign authors who, either by prolonged personal contact or through the popularity and availability of their writings, usually in translation, exerted a literally incalculable influence upon English thought. Johan Boemus gave considerable attention to the putative early history of man in his widely read *Omnium gentium mores.*[15] Shocked by the contemporary spectacle of Christian princes fighting each other for reasons alien to the *philosophia Christi,* Erasmus was moved to make what was for him a rare foray into historical speculation concerning man's early social evolution.[16] Juan Luis Vives, who lived for more continuous time in England than Erasmus, made such speculations an integral part of his extensive critique of contemporary learning.[17] And, if Elizabethan readers were as familiar as it appears they were with the work of Louis LeRoy, they could have found in his *Vicissitudes,* as translated by Robert Ashley, a still more detailed, and a more radically secular, reconstruction.[18]

Out of the writings of these authors there emerges a more or less consistent picture of man's early existence, one that implied a reasonable hypothesis and, though of course imaginary, at least accorded with experience. It was far from original, to be sure. Like the more restricted idea of man's beginnings in forest and field, this reconstruction of his subsequent development up to the formation of social organization and governments still depended on classical models, of which Aristotle's was surely the best known.[19] Its authors approached their subject developmentally. From an isolated existence, lacking all the relationships and amenities of civilized life, people eventually found protection and satisfaction in progressively complex organizations until, with the formation of lawmaking governments, their society may be said to have moved from prehistory to history. Meanwhile they were gaining in practical wisdom and in their mastery of their environment, moving from foraging for roots and acorns to husbandry and the arts. Though the religious sense was most likely to be held part of man's nature,[20] there were those who maintained that man's spiritual needs had to wait until his material wants had been satisfied.[21] It had all, in any case, been a natural process, one that took place "in the course of time" and in response to necessity or opportunity.[22]

Not the least of the insights into the life of early man that bear relation to the cave myth is perception of language as an aspect of social evolution. The idea was hardly new. It was in fact an integral part of the cave myth as elaborated by classical authors.[23] In contrast to the biblical story in which Adam was empowered to give ready-made names to all creatures, the classical tradition pictured mankind having gradually to put sounds together into words that stood for things and thus to achieve in the long run a coherent language. This interpretation continued to satisfy most Renaissance writers, but some were able to go one hesitant, but important, step beyond the assumption that words arose simply to designate things toward the more modern perception of language as a function of community and meaning as a function of use. "Daily business," wrote Vives, "brought men together, and speech bound them to move as closely as possible amongst one another in an indivisible perpetual society."[24] According to venerable tradition, poets were especially responsible for creating the conditions essential to a community of this sort. Puttenham found them "the original cause and occasion of . . . [the] first assemblies, when before people remained in woods and mountains, vagrant and dispersed like wild beasts."[25] And William Webbe declared that it was by means of poetry, "by the force of this measured and tuneful speaking," that people were "brought to civility and gentleness and right knowledge."[26]

But whatever weight they may have assigned to the factors of use and community, what most impressed those who resorted to the cave myth about the origins of language was its gradualness and naturalness. On the basis of what he had learned about New World barbarism, Richard Eden generalized that all tongues were once "barbarous and needy," and that "in the first age of the world" people "had a short language of a few words."[27] According to Puttenham, language evolved slowly in accordance with man's ability to speak, to use, that is, the unique anatomy of his throat which enabled him to utter a wide variety of sounds, an ability that made him "more disciplinable and imaginative than any other creature."[28]

The cave myth, it must be kept in mind, was only one of several myths of origin that reflected Renaissance England's perception of prehistory. So it is necessary to study it to some extent in relation to those other myths, the most important of which being the Mosaic account of man's beginnings, the euhemeristic mythology, the myth of a past Golden Age, and its correlative, the myth of universal decline.

As long as the authors mentioned above followed the lead of their classical sources, they managed to agree on a more or less consistent and confessionally neutral reconstruction of man's earliest condition. But no matter how committed they may have been to the cave myth, they remained still more committed to the Christian story and, in particular, to the first eleven chapters of Genesis—as, of course, elaborated by the commentators. Most would probably have agreed with Bodin, who qualified his essentially naturalistic explanation of social evolution by declaring that he placed Moses "ahead of all the writings and opinions of all philosophers."[29] Conflict would seem consequently to have been unavoidable. The Mosaic story and the cave myth did, after all, differ in essence—the former purporting to be the Word of God directed toward a particular people, the latter the speculation of pagan authors upon their own perception of the human condition; the former theocentric, the latter anthropocentric.

The account of man's initial existence, as adapted from classical sources, has in fact no real counterpart in the text of Genesis. Starting, as they did, from scratch, Adam's progeny were a very different breed from the quasi-feral creatures envisioned in most versions of the cave myth. The Mosaic account proceeds directly from their tilling of the soil to Cain's building of a city. With a similar economy of word and idea, subsequent innovations in cattle raising, metallurgy, and the making of musical instruments are confined to three verses[30] and are clearly incidental to the primarily genealogical purposes of the Hebrew poet. In contrast to typical evocations of the cave myth, which name no names whether of gods or men, this laconic reference to cultural innovation left no room for anything so impersonal as the social evolution that marked man's initial conquest of his environment in the more extended versions of the cave myth.

Yet overt conflict between the two versions was for the most part avoided. This was partly because Renaissance minds were notoriously capable of thinking on apparently divergent lines with no sense of incongruity, but mainly because the two traditions could be made to seem not so very far apart. The cave myth could be taken simply as a secular gloss upon a text left sketchy by the Hebrew poet. Take Adam and his progeny out of the context of sacred history, and their situation could be seen as at least parallel to that of the cave and forest dwellers. Both had to make their way by the sweat of their faces. As Genesis was expanded by a succession of commentators more than willing to reconcile it with classical sources, discrepancies tended to shrink.[31] And, if the pagan deities gave too much trouble, they could be, and increasingly were, passed off as corruptions of biblical personages.

But for the catastrophic fact of the Fall, which all assumed as given no matter how literally they may have rendered the substance of the cave myth, it was even possible, after a fashion, to conflate the two versions. Thomas Wilson, the rhetorician, insisted on interpreting the cave myth itself in providential terms, considering the subsequent rise of civilization as a restoration to man by God's grace rather than as man's own response to the circumstances of his secular existence.[32] The cosmographer, Peter Heylyn, argued that the contribution made by Cain and his get to man's early condition proved that God had purposely left man to his own resources of "judgment, wit, and understanding" in order to provide for his natural needs.[33] On the other hand, while working mainly from biblical and scholastic sources rather than from classical ones, Richard Hooker arrived at an anthropology that differed little from that inherent in the cave myth.[34]

The confusion that a dual approach could nevertheless create is especially well exemplified by one author of the early sixteenth century whose writings reverberated in English thought for generations following.[35] Like most of his contemporaries who had anything to say about the human condition, Johann Boemus felt he had to begin his *Omnium gentium mores* at the very beginning. But he found himself faced with divergent authorities: on the one hand, the "true opinions of the divine writers" and, on the other, "the vain fantasies of the ethnics." In view of the obvious discrepancies between the two traditions, he tried his best to convey the essence of the cave myth in biblical terms, though at some cost to the classical story and to chronological clarity. "The rude simplicity of the first world," described essentially in terms of the cave myth, lasted, he said, from Adam to the Flood "and many years after." In the familiar process by which people moved from isolation to community, seeking to avoid a competitive war of each against all, "like wild beasts," they did so well for a while as to create something like the Garden of Eden, a place in which they "might have been called gods" but for the intervention of Satan and the rise of idolatry.[36]

Unsatisfactory as this forced marriage of classical and biblical tradition may have been, there was more trouble to come. On the ultimate origins of the universe and man, Boemus had still to deal with the more radical of the ethnics' "vain fantasies," no matter how vain they may have been. He had to deal in particular with the idea, apparently adapted from the Lucretian version of Epicurean cosmology,[37] that described how the variety of living forms, including man, had emerged as a natural result of the sun's heat acting upon an initially uniform body of water by a "proportionate tempering of moisture and heat." This hypothesis, like the still more fundamental speculation of Lucretius concerning the atomic origin of all matter, continued to trouble orthodox scholars for a long time. In the mid-seventeenth century, the very orthodox Stillingfleet was still combatting the Lucretian hypothesis, paying it a left-handed compliment as the origin theory "which makes most noise in the world."[38] Boemus, himself, seems to have found it both repellent and fascinating. He certainly spent a disproportionate amount of time on it. The fact of immediate importance, however, is that, once he had demolished it by the authority of the "divine writers," a more or less standard version of the theologically neutral cave myth was left standing, ready to perform its usual service as a rational and secular supplement to the story the

Mosaic poet had left sketchy and cryptic—which is all it was ordinarily meant to be.

The cave myth in fact remained subtly secular, both in essence and influence. It fitted in with the propensity of English humanists for treating human problems primarily in the light of human history and, by providing a quasi-historical model for doing so, no doubt encouraged this tendency. Despite their obvious dedication to the life of the spirit, the most Christian of Tudor Christian humanists were able to view the history of civilization without necessary or constant reference to the theology of history. The cave myth in effect bypassed both Genesis and the pagan mythology without overtly challenging either. But the prevailing tendency of those who resorted to it for more than rhetorical purposes was to explore its implications within the context of secondary rather than final causes. Even Ralegh, painfully conscious of Providence as the ultimate arbiter in human affairs, and wary of giving undue weight to second causes, found it necessary to explain human actions as far as possible in terms of reason and experience.[39] And LeRoy's English readers could find in the early pages of his *De la vicissitude* an account which, but for the assertion of an inborn sense of religion, told the story of man's emergence from the caves with no reference to divine intervention of any kind.[40]

The cave myth was to prove even more difficult to square with the euhemerist orthodoxy than with the Christian. On the crucial issue of invention, euhemerism stood in direct opposition to it. The pagan invention myths, like the Mosaic, turned upon the catastrophic acts of individuals, the cave myth upon the gradual and incremental contribution of unnamed generations, made in response to environmental necessity.[41]

Necessity, indeed, figures largely in Elizabeth comments on man's earliest condition. While not ruling out the possibility of catastrophic invention, or intervention by the technic gods of euhemerist tradition, necessity fitted better with the anonymous gradualism implied in the cave myth. Elizabethans were ready to believe, with Aristotle, that necessity was the mother of invention.[42] As relayed to English readers by Ashley, LeRoy's account of man's earliest state stressed necessity to the total exclusion of the inventive deities: Prometheus appears in it, but only in passing and strictly as a metaphor for the efforts of real but anonymous people to gain knowledge. With mention of such names as Democritus and Aristotle, it becomes clear that by then, and only then, man's story has emerged from the mists of prehistory.[43]

This is not to say that the exponents of the cave myth had to make a clear choice and to challenge the classical tradition outright. Such a confrontation had to wait until the eighteenth century. Typically eclectic, they simply added to their intellectual stock-in-trade a myth that explained more of what they wanted to have explained.

That Renaissance English authors who had something to say about their own culture chose from their classical heritage as a point of departure the dismal picture of early man as a creature of necessity rather than the very durable tradition that pictured him as living a life of happy simplicity is, in itself, a matter of considerable significance. Their classical sources provided ample material for either choice, though the cave myth seems to have predominated in later writings.[44] The Hesiodic vision of the Golden Age—the age of Saturn that, thanks to Jupiter's machinations, declined into an age of iron—remained a popular tradition, especially among those moralists who distrusted the arts as well as the desire for knowledge and power over nature that risked the anger of the jealous gods. The opposite view arose out of a belief, no doubt rooted in the folk memory but validated by observation of contemporary barbarism, that life had in fact improved since the days when people scrambled for a living in the primeval wilderness. These two myths had one thing in common, however—namely the presumed simplicity of man's initial condition: whereas the one might idealize the simple life, the other might stress its stark limitations. The cave myth and that of a past age of gold nevertheless represented for classical authors opposite poles of the mythopoeic imagination.

And they continued to do so for English authors. The cave myth appealed to those who were concerned with the known course of civilization and who were animated by a faith in man's ability to realize the potential inherent in his "excellent nature." The Golden Age belonged rather to the realm of Platonic ideas. It bore no necessary relation to historical time. It could be past, present, or future—in its most inspirational form it could be identified with a cyclical return, of Astraea, for example, or of Arthur. It appealed especially to the nostalgia of poets and moralists and to their elegiac or Arcadian sensibilities. The Golden Age, and its grim relative the myth of universal degeneration, represented, however, an inveterate cast of mind, a mentality that students of real history could not wholly ignore. By virtue of the analogy it bore to the Mosaic myth of a lost paradise, the Golden Age was easy to reconcile with sacred history, especially for those commentators who were themselves steeped in classical traditions.[45] And the related myth of universal decay derived additional sanction from biblical history and Christian eschatology.

In view of the strength of the rival traditions, it is the more remarkable that English writers of the Tudor period chose the cave myth with such consistency. By doing so, they made a decision that was more far reaching than they no doubt realized. Their choice, it is true, was not a clear matter of either/or: Renaissance minds were, as we have had reason to notice in more than one context, quite capable of at the very least paying lip service to apparently irreconcilable positions. Even as convinced a believer in the cave myth as Thomas Starkey could not help slipping back into the rhetorical formula of the Golden Age.[46] But, by seizing so happily upon the more rigorous tradition, he and his like-minded contemporaries were able to escape both the only thinly veiled pessimism inherent in the Golden Age tradition and the more obvious pessimism inherent in the related theory of the decay of nature.

The optimistic character of the cave myth is important, for optimism and pessimism maintained a discordant balance in that age of dramatic contrasts,[47] the former responding to the vision of an apparently rational universe, a world of expanding opportunity and the prospect of a new science, the latter to a distrust of the very changes that inspired the former, to a neurotic sense of mutability, to a feeling that coherence had somehow gone from the world picture, and to a reading of Scripture that held out little promise for life in this world. The myth of a Golden Age caused less overt opposition than the assumption of universal degeneration, and for the simple reason that golden ages have little to do with history, whereas the vision of man and nature in a state of irreversible decline, supported both by tradition and a perverse reading of experience, became in itself a philosophy of history. Heirs to the humanist tradition, however, were capable of giving short shrift to the notion of a past age of gold. Sir Thomas Smith, as trustworthy a spokesman as any for Elizabethan humanism, rejected outright the idea that the earliest age had been especially virtuous and, in line with the cave myth, maintained that it was in fact "uncultivated and devoid of learning."[48] And Bodin's English readers could well have noticed his scorn for the maniacal violence and debauchery of the Hesiodic pantheon, and for a so-called Golden Age "in which men were scattered like beasts in the fields and the woods and had as much as they could keep by means of force and crime"[49]—a condition that in fact differed little from that envisioned in the cave myth itself.

The myth of universal decay, on the other hand, was made of tougher stuff, for it became a central issue in the climactic Quarrel of the Ancients and Moderns. Always a favorite theme of preachers and moralists, it permeated much of the thought devoted to the earliest times. Scholars took it for granted that any migration of ideas, customs, or language must represent a process of deterioration. Stillingfleet, as we have seen, assumed without question that pagan mythology in particular evolved as a corruption of the original "Scripture-history." But the developmental optimism that was both cause and effect of the cave myth prevailed in the long run. George Hakewill proved more than a match for the conservative Godfrey Goodman in their memorable encounter, and the Baconian faith in the capacity of the mind, once properly equipped, was vindicated in the ultimate victory of the Moderns.[50]

From what has gone before, it should be apparent that the significance the cave myth bore for historical thought derives primarily from its developmental implications, especially the perspective it provided for an evolutionary view of the history of civilization. Perceptions of social evolution long preceded those involving the biological order, and it was then relatively safe to give expression to them. Unlike any theory that questioned the fixity of species, the perception of social development did not directly contradict Genesis, nor were those who found inspiration in the vision of man's rise from a state of savagery as yet trying to elaborate a formal philosophy of history out of it, no matter how much the concept may in fact have been conditioning their historical thought. The developmental implications of the cave myth did not, of course, encompass the unlimited and inevitable progress envisioned by later evolutionary theorists. Any implications of progress that might inhere in the frequent observations of the progress actually made by mankind, and in the cave myth itself, must, in any case, be viewed in relation to the competing perception of historical cycles, the still prevalent notion of the decay of nature, the consciousness of Original Sin, and the time scheme prescribed by Christian eschatology.

Nevertheless, to say, as has been said, that there are no ideas of progress to be found through the Renaissance[51] is to overlook not only the developmental implications associated with the various uses to which the cave myth was put, but those statements referred to in a previous chapter that rejected the idea of invention as a catastrophic act, presumably by some person or deity, in favor of the steady, incremental, and for the most part anonymous contributions made over the ages to the evolution of society.[52] Man's progressive control of his environment had been apparent since ancient times to anyone who cared to notice: the march of civilization may not have been in a straight line—both ancients and moderns were only too aware of the ups and down, the slumps and returns, that had actually taken place—but march it unquestionably had. And, by virtue of the implications it bore of development and relativity, that perception was preparing the way for, was indeed already involved in, the revolution in historical consciousness which rescued Western thought from the idea of an absolute natural law and an essentially static view of society.

Renaissance England was well prepared to appreciate that process, and, in particular, to reconstruct the early history of man in terms of social evolution. Events in that period of more than ordinarily radical transition had fostered an unprecedented sensitivity to change. In traditional institutions—in church, in government, in law, in the circumstances of daily life, in the language itself—the fact of change was unavoidable. Change also perplexed observers hitherto accustomed to assuming a body politic of established order in which alteration was reflected only in its health, not its structure. To such observers, to the Tudor humanist-publicists, for example, in their earnest search for the causes of social and cultural maladjustment, the evidence of change led naturally enough to the past, ultimately to the most distant past imaginable within the parameters of reason and experience—which is to say, to the myth of man's solitary and exiguous existence in a primeval wilderness. By reversing direction, the cave myth could become a logical point of departure for an interpretation of history in terms of an apparent progression from the simple to the complex.

That interpretation made possible a guarded optimism. Boemus had declared it his purpose in surveying the customs of the world to show how, despite the machinations of the devil, "men in these days have amended the rude simplicity of the first world."[53] On the basis of biblical tradition, Hooker expressed a similar optimism. Though well aware of "the hastiness of our wills" and the indelible fact of Original Sin, he asked his readers only to compare their own times with those "wherein there were no civil societies . . . wherein there was as yet no manner of public regiment established . . . wherein there were not above eight persons righteous living upon the face of the earth: and we have surely good cause to think that God hath blessed us exceedingly."[54]

As Starkey's use of the cave myth indicates, optimism stemmed not only from observation but from a profound assumption concerning the mind of man as expressed in the epistemology of the tabula rasa. As Hooker put it, "the soul of man being therefore at the first as a book, wherein nothing is and yet all things may be emprinted; we are to search by what steps and degrees it riseth into perfection of knowledge." Unlike Starkey, he denied that virtue was inborn: "For into the world we come . . . as naked in mind as in body."[55] Richard Eden found that the same principle applied to contemporary savagery, and with the same implications of potentiality. With the somewhat romantic early reports from the New World in mind, he likened "these simple gentiles" living after the law of nature "to a smooth and bare tablet unpainted, or a white paper unwritten on," and therefore capable of receiving any imprint.[56]

The image of contemporary savagery and the cave myth obviously had much in common. Both seemed to exemplify an elemental primitivism, the one reinforcing notions entertained about the other. Assuming the psychic unity of mankind, and proceeding on the basis of uncritically perceived similarities between past and present-day societies, those interested in the history of mankind could convince themselves that the savage peoples of the New World, the barbarians of antiquity, the Greeks themselves in their early days, even the early inhabitants of Britain, to say nothing of the contemporary "wild" Irish who so shocked (and fascinated)

English proconsuls—all shared a primitive life-style, a common childhood that placed them in a similar process of cultural development.[57] It was a process, however, that took place not according to the linear temporal sequence from the Creation to the present favored by most chronographers, but in response to the varying circumstances of time and place. The savage might still have to be placed in the chain of being, but, in the light of what was becoming known about primitive peoples, the chain itself had to be reinterpreted in temporal terms rather than as the static expression of an absolute natural law.[58]

In this respect, it would be hard to overestimate the importance of the voyages of discovery, and in particular the perceptions of life among the American Indians they made possible. Better than the imaginary peoples conventionally pictured in the cave myth, the Indians appeared to represent the reality of primitive savagery, "an example of the life of our first parents."[59] Though Arcadian values at times crept into reports that pictured the Indians as living simply, without laws or anxiety for the future, a state somewhere between the savagery of the cave myth and the idealism of the Golden Age, Elizabethan England for the most part imagined them as wild and feral: the "noble savage" had yet to make his presence felt in English thought.

During the later Elizabethan years, and especially during the ensuing century, comparing the American aborigines with early peoples, including those hypothetical dwellers in the primeval caves and forests, became a commonplace. Ralegh made such likenesses an element of the anthropology that is secreted in the interstices of his world history. Citing both "Vespucius" and "ancient stories," he concluded that all peoples after the Flood were very like American Indians.[60] In the more specialized context of literary criticism, George Puttenham undertook to prove that rhyme was "an instinct of nature" by citing both ancient custom and travelers who reported that "the American, the Perusine, and the very Cannibal" sang "their highest and holiest matters in rhyming versicles."[61] Similarly, LeRoy found that an inborn desire for religion could be demonstrated by travelers who found peoples "living as the first men," without arts, letters, or laws, yet not without religion.[62]

Renaissance readers did not, it is true, really need the spectacle of American savagery to document the cave myth. Awareness of stages of savagery and barbarism was at least as old as Herodotus. Contemporaries of Pliny and Diodorus, comfortable in their own ethnocentricity, had enjoyed highly colored reports of strange and uncouth peoples. Such reports continued to be read for centuries thereafter, and with similar enjoyment and credulity. And medieval lore added so much that was still more fabulous and preposterous as to make the American Indians look only "a bit odd" by comparison.[63] Savagery, moreover, had enjoyed a life of its own in folklore and symbol. Wild men had long lurked in the forests that rimmed the world of the medieval imagination. For the Elizabethan Spenser, they could still symbolize man's unregenerate nature.[64] But theirs was a savagery unrelated to time, a literary device. It in fact took the news from the New World to bring the European mind back to reality, and, in the process, to give the classical anthropology of the cave a new credibility.

What brought the perception of savagery as a stage in a process of social evolution home to English minds with peculiar poignancy was the realization that their own ancestors were at one time more like the American Indians—or, for that matter, the primitives they envisioned in their versions of the cave myth—than the more or less conventionally and anachronistically accoutered heroes of national legend. In the 1520s, John Twyne had made the connection between the ancient Britons and the cave myth, but only by a realistic reading of the Roman histories.[65] By the early years of the seventeenth century, that perception had absorbed the additional support available in the American experience. By then the connection between the Indians and the early Britons had become explicit in the illustrations appended to John Speed's *History of Great Britain,* which pictured the latter as indeed naked, painted, and by any standard savage.[66]

It remains to be asked what relationship there may have been between the cave myth and the more formal and sophisticated political thinking of the period, in particular the concept of a presocial "state of nature" that served as a baseline for much of the political discourse during the revolutionary decades of the early seventeenth century. During the preceding century, the cave myth had remained an idea loaded with implications that were seldom clearly articulated, an idea that stimulated thought but gave little direction to it. Tudor England was not, to be sure, much given to theorizing about the nature of political society beyond the politico-ecclesiastical controversies, and even then systematic formulation had to await Hooker's monumental *Laws of Ecclesiastical Polity*. As the revolutionary period approached, however, issues arose that demanded, and received, theoretical attention of the utmost sophistication. Though by no means irrelevant to such discussion, the simple historical anthropology of the classical cave myth was no longer able, as such, to contribute to it; nor, in particular, was it able to claim real identity with the hypothesized state of nature on which English theorists, from Hobbes to Locke, anchored their systems.

That there was a relationship between the two, however, is obvious, but what that relationship was is not. In a sense, the cave myth may be considered to have evolved into the state of nature theory while losing its initial identity in the process. The theorists of the revolutionary era needed a logical, if not a historical, starting point as much as their Tudor predecessors; and the tendency to start with something like the classical myth had become habitual. Whether the human condition as it was perceived to have existed before the advent of social organization was a beastly one or merely a state of benign simplicity depended on the exigencies of controversy, but in either case it bore similarities to the historical mythology of classical antiquity that are surely more than coincidental.

Although the state of nature as it appears in English political discussion represented an essentially secular mythology roughly congruent with that of the classical cave myth, something functionally similar to it arose out of a scholastic background in the form of the revived Thomist-Aristotelian natural law theory of the sixteenth century,[67] a tradition interpreted for seventeenth-century England by Richard Hooker.

As developed by Hooker, that tradition embodied something that was for practical purposes like the cave myth but based on a historical anthropology derived more from biblical than classical sources. Hooker's neo-Aristotelianism allowed him, it is true, to assume that society was natural in its origin and purpose, but his conception of man's natural state before the advent of social organization came straight out of the Book of Genesis.[68] For that reason, it represented for him an unimpeachably historical reality, not merely a logical necessity. But it was a different reality from that which exponents of the classical myth had in mind. It involved initially the Adamic family rather than the anonymous denizens of the primeval countryside, and, though Adam and his progeny were hardly above reproach, they were certainly not beastlike. Yet, as it develops, Hooker's reconstruction of the origins of political society reveals much in common with the classical myth as it had been expressed by Thomas Starkey a century before. Fallen man was from the beginning prone to evil as well as to good, and he lacked in "the first age" those things needful for a life "fit for the dignity of man." He was nevertheless capable of acting rationally to remedy those deficiencies, and, as families multiplied, and the problems inherent in his unregenerate nature multiplied with them, he was able to seek protection in political society, "as the law of nature doth require." Though programmed, as it were, by nature, man was at first very much on his own. His mind being "at the first as a book, wherein nothing is, and yet all things may be imprinted,"[69] he was capable, as Starkey had maintained, of adjusting to and shaping his environment. And if anyone doubted that things were then better than now, let him just imagine a time when there was no "civil society" or "public regiment," and when "Seth, Enoch, and those few the rest in that line" were the only righteous living on earth.[70]

For Hooker, the presocial human condition, the state of "mere natural man,"[71] was clearly historical. For later theorists who may have been inspired by his rationalism, if not by the scholasticism out of which it arose, the historical status of their state of nature is by no means so clear. Nor is the lingering shadow of the cave myth. That the latter was there is hardly contestable. Not only had it permeated the vocabulary of political discourse, but, as seventeenth-century thought became more than ever conscious of the primitive peoples of the New World, it even gained a certain degree of verisimilitude. Hobbes' famous conclusion that life in the state of nature was "solitary, poor, nasty, brutish and short" comes consequently as no surprise.[72]

Whether Hobbes' state of nature was a logical necessity for him or a historical reality is debatable.[73] It no doubt represented not so much what man's life in the first age must have been as what it would have been had all law, including the means of contract enforcement, been absent—to say nothing of the arts and letters and the commodities of civilized existence. In which case, it would surely be logical to assume that life would have been cursed by the chronic conflict "of every man against every man"—an eventuality which, however, Hobbes conceded "never was generally so, over all the world."[74] His state of nature may from this point of view be considered rather a commentary on human nature than on human history.

But it is easy to exaggerate the ahistorical character of Hobbes' state of nature. He was quite capable of thinking in both philosophical and historical terms, and his description of the human condition in the first age shows signs of a genetic relationship to those habits of thought that were traditionally expressed in the cave myth. He added to his admission that the war of each against all was never "generally so" the further qualification that it might still be found "in many places of America." And he reflected the antiquarian scholarship of the preceding hundred years (perhaps, indeed, that of Camden)[75] when, at another point, he wrote that the primitive state of war is borne out not only "by the experience of savage nations that live at this day" but "by the histories of our ancestors the old inhabitants of Germany, and other now civil countries, where we find the people few, and short-lived, and without the ornaments and comforts of life, which by peace and society are usually invented and procured."[76] That Hobbes found it necessary to assume a state of nature for the sake of argument is not, then, bound to mean that it was utterly ahistorical, or that he did not also retain in the back of his mind the pregnant premise of the cave myth. On the contrary, his recourse to a state of nature could mean simply that he shared the faith nourished by so many of his predecessors in the virtues of a historical perspective that reached its ultimate point in the prehistory of man.

The cave myth provided Renaissance England with its most useful, and, insofar as it accorded with observable data, its most realistic perception of man's earliest existence. Though highly imaginative, based upon the adaptation of an ancient idea to contemporary concerns rather than upon empirical investigation, and seldom given systematic expression, it nevertheless served better than its classical models—better, too, at least for secular purposes, than the Mosaic mythology—the need felt by historically minded people naively bent on finding authority and a sense of stability in the most distant antiquity. Seemingly validated by experience, it allowed those interested to search beyond history's limits into the penumbra of prehistory. Avoiding the antidevelopmental myths of a golden age and of universal decay, as well as the euhemerist invention myths, those who resorted to the cave myth were able to arrive at what for practical purposes amounted to a coherent anthropology—one, moreover, that, by bypassing both pagan divinity and sacred history without overtly challenging either, in effect achieved a theologically neutral view of prehistory. The cave myth thus served symbolically, and to an extent impossible to measure objectively, as a bridge of sorts between providential history and the perception of an evolving civilization, between the ambivalent skepticism and fickle rationalism of the Renaissance years and the more systematic skepticism and more confident rationalism of the eighteenth century.

5

The British History: The Problem of Legend

Mists also shrouded England's most distant antiquity, but they were not so hard to penetrate as those that obscured the earliest history of mankind. In contrast to the historicity of the Olympian deities, which was as hard to prove as to disprove and prompted little formal debate before the eighteenth century, that of the nation's founders and early heroes became the subject of substantive and ultimately decisive controversy. The result provides a classic opportunity to study the process by which belief was beginning to give way to skepticism. The legend of Britain's founding by Brutus and his Trojan followers and the stories of early Britain's greatest hero King Arthur became in fact the twin subjects of a long and bitter battle of books that lasted for over a century. Though hardly a major affair as controversy in the Reformation century went, it nevertheless represented a crisis of belief that brought the tension between belief and skepticism into sharper focus than had as yet been possible in the case of the ancient myth history.

The national legendary history, as is surely well known, came down to Tudor readers from Geoffrey of Monmouth's *Historia regum Britanniae* (c. 1135) as part of a continued history known as the *Brut*. Published for the first time by Caxton and republished throughout the ensuing century, the *Brut* constituted what for most English readers passed for the nation's prehistory. It relayed Geoffrey's story of Brutus, a Trojan leader who, after the fall of Troy, worked his way up through Western Europe until he finally reached the British Isles, where he encountered and overcame an indigenous race of giants and founded a dynasty that reached its culmination, and disastrous end, in the brilliant reign of King Arthur.

The appeal of Geoffrey's book (now generally accepted as largely the product of his own imagination) is understandable. It told a good story and provided successive generations of English readers with what passed for a respectable national beginning—like their Gallic neighbors, the English found the idea of their own descent from a band of wandering exiles oddly inspiring. And, in the Arthurian tales, Geoffrey provided not only lots of action typical of early chivalry but, more significant for the purposes of the Tudor mythology, something that combined history and romance in a way that continued to inspire the imagination of patriotic writers long after historical scholarship had begun clearly to distinguish between the two. In Arthur himself, Geoffrey created a world-class hero who, as conqueror of everything around him, as well as founder of the famous Round Table, provided propagandists, pageant makers, and poets with a constant source of material, a symbolism further enhanced by the myth of his prophesied return. Arthur's reputation in sixteenth-century England rested, however, more on his portrayal as a national hero and conqueror than on his personification of the chivalric ideal.[1]

These stories had long been cherished, and sometimes criticized, but it was not until Henry VIII's reign that the stage was set for a major controversy over their historicity. Controversy would surely have come sooner or later—the legends contained too much fancy for the skeptical, yet more than enough patriotic appeal to fortify the still widespread will to believe. The early decades of the sixteenth century in fact witnessed a confluence of factors that determined the incidence and character of the ensuing controversy.

For one thing, early Tudor England was becoming more than ever sensitive about its history. In addition to the authority then generally ascribed to origins, indeed to mere antiquity, there existed a very practical need for the prestige that a national pedigree was thought to convey. In the increasingly competitive world of diplomacy, prestige depended to a degree now hard to imagine upon just such an ability to trace national history to the utmost antiquity, to legendary founders, even to the figures of ancient myth and sacred history. The Trojan legend was able to link both: the pedigree of Brutus led back to the demigods through his great grandfather, Aeneas, and ultimately to Saturn himself. If Britain's eponymous heroes were hardly demigods, their treatment by the legendeers of medieval and Renaissance England bore interesting parallels to the euhemerist process. And, in the interest of public relations, English monarchs were almost as ready as their Continental contemporaries to have themselves identified with such figures as Hercules, or, in the case of Elizabeth, with Diana or Astraea. Like their contemporaries, too, both Henry VII and Henry VIII pursued their public diplomacy in an atmosphere of pageantry and symbolism in which the shadow of legend had routinely to pass for the substance of history.[2]

However, happy as the Tudor pageant masters may have been to use the legends and the court to encourage them, the court was not the source of the controversy over their historicity. Like their predecessors, Renaissance politicians tended to be pragmatic about such things; a good story, one that served a good purpose, could not be a bad story regardless of its lack of historical truth. And anyway, it is easy to overestimate the seriousness with which either Henry took the propagandist use made of the legends, especially the Arthurian theme. Henry VII no doubt saw the advantage of calling attention to his own Welsh background when he named his eldest son Arthur, but the curriculum he had Bernard André draw up for the boy's education contained none of the traditional Arthurian material. Although he had in hand, in the form of the *Brut,* a national history that incorporated the legends of Brutus and Arthur and the rest of Geoffrey's mischievous legacy, he chose to import an Italian humanist, Polydore Vergil, whose historical perspective, solidly grounded in the classics, was unlikely to extend into the obscurity of British antiquity. Henry VIII, moreover, continued to support Polydore Vergil after he had been attacked by partisans of Geoffrey; nor, on the other hand, did Elizabeth take any action against critics of the sacred legendary history.

Nevertheless, it was the upsurge of patriotism inspired by the Tudor dynasty that became a precondition essential to the historical debate. This peculiarly Tudor patriotism naturally found its most fervent, certainly its most vocal, exponents among writers of Welsh background. But a similarly touchy patriotism characterized others of the scholarly community. John Rastell, humanist and member of the More circle, condemned one of the fabulous stories that clung to the main stem of the legendary history on the ground not only that it was, indeed, preposterous, but that it might cause "other people" to "laugh us to scorn."[3] And John Bale was so shocked at the irresponsible dispersal of the monastic libraries, and so concerned over the possibility that "the monuments" of England's history might find their way into the hands of foreign collectors, that he proposed the establishment of a national library.[4] Those partisans who rose to the defense of Geoffrey had no monopoly on patriotism, however. They were simply more vocal in their expression of it. Patriotic sentiment nevertheless supplied the combustible stuff that made an outbreak possible.

Bale's use of the Samothes legend will show to what lengths a patriotic will to believe could go in an effort to fill in the blank spaces in the nation's early history. Though he squandered much of his talents on an antipapal campaign of unparalleled scurrility, Bale was a man of extensive learning and some originality as a historian.[5] But in order to complete a line of rulers of England that reached back to Noah, he used the spurious account of postdiluvian history published by Annius of Viterbo in 1498. Though the Pseudo-Berosus was questioned as early as 1522, it had not yet been proven false, and Bale considered the Chaldean sage on a par with Moses as an authority. With its help, he managed to inject into his historical scheme a certain Samothes, a figure supposed to be a son of Japhet and grandson of Noah. Somehow this man ended up in Britain, where he taught the Britons knowledge of astronomy and the science of politics, and founded a line of kings, all more or less imaginary, who lasted till the arrival of Albion, a wicked giant. This son of Neptune and heir to the Egyptian line of Isis and Osiris inaugurated a bad period for Britain and made it possible to account for the savage race of giants which, according to Geoffrey, Brutus and his followers found upon their arrival in Britain.[6] Such was the will to believe a story that would fill in the intolerable gaps in the nation's genealogy that the Samothes legend (not incidentally part of the *Brut*) was told and retold by otherwise reputable chroniclers to the end of the century.[7]

The antiquarian activity that provided much of the substance and method for the controversy over the British History was itself an expression of Tudor patriotism. The Tudor century witnessed the advent of a new kind of scholar, devoted to the history and topography—to the chorography, that is—of their own country. Not quite accepted as historians nor given to calling themselves historians, and always capable of lapsing into parochialism and mere curiosity hunting, this new breed in fact did more to open up the social and cultural past to English minds than did conventional historians, most of whom still acted on the assumption that history consisted primarily of past politics.[8] The British History controversy was both a cause of their activity and a result of it: antiquarians raised the issue in the first place, and the debate gave them the chance to develop a movement that was to culminate in the relatively mature antiquarian scholarship of Camden. The preceding century had seen some movement in this same direction, but it was not until John Leland undertook his pioneering "itineraries" that chorographical investigation—and speculation—began in earnest, and, in a more obscure but complementary way, John Twyne, the Canterbury schoolmaster and humanist, showed how speculative antiquarianism could cast the obliquely revealing light of hypothesis and reasoned conjecture on early societies.[9]

The advent of humanism was to this activity, as to most others in the intellectual life of Tudor England, a precondition pervasively effective. It had sunk roots in England during the fifteenth century, but did not flower until the sixteenth. By then it was permeating English culture, reforming secular education, giving direction to scholarship, and shaping historical thought. Though English humanism embodied the classical orientation and the faith in the philological method typical of the humanist scholarship imported from Italy, it tended to be applied to problems of society rather than to pure scholarship. One of those problems—though a lesser one, to be sure—turned out to be that concerning the early history of England. While no one involved in that controversy escaped the influence of this new learning, it worked more to the advantage of the critics than to the supporters of the Galfridean tradition, for it fostered a relatively critical, demystifying attitude toward tradition, whereas it was tradition that the conservatives were committed to support. Humanism may perhaps have contributed something else, namely a sense of the absurd, the ironical mind-set of the More of *Utopia,* for example, or of the Erasmus of the *Praise of Folly.* Even those who were perfectly willing to accept euhemerist explanations of their own origins, or of origins in general—Polydore Vergil himself, for example—could look with a satirical eye on the patriotic pretensions inherent in the Brutus story.[10]

Now the preconditions mentioned above interacted with some complexity, nor did they always point in the same direction. Patriotic fervor and the mind-set of humanism did not have to be at odds and fortunately for the most part were not, but they could be; and the tendencies inherent in humanist historical thought toward rationalism, and, in particular, toward bringing tradition into accord with reason and experience, could work in opposite ways. On the one hand, those scholars and men of letters closest to the humanist community, while as patriotic as anyone else, naturally tended to view the distant past rather in the perspective of classical antiquity than in that of the native tradition represented by the *Brut.* On the other hand those who felt more comfortable with the medieval tradition, antiquaries of Welsh backgound, for example, though by no means unschooled in the substance and method of humanism, turned those resources toward support of that tradition. For them, a patriotic compulsion to believe and to rationalize the irrational tended to overpower scholarly insight. It was not patriotism per se but a deeply offended patriotism that made these authors capable of reacting with unwonted ferocity to anyone who questioned that tradition, especially if from the perspective of classical authority.

This, of course, is exactly what happened, and it is this that touched off the battle of books. In 1534, Polydore Vergil finally published the history of England he had been commissioned by Henry VII to write and on which he had been working for years. Polydore had the disadvantage of being a foreigner and, after the break with Rome, a Catholic. But when he not only charged that Geoffrey's account of the origin of Britain lacked respectable authority but suggested as well that it was contrary to common sense and a bit ridiculous to boot,[11] he pulled the house down on himself. He continued to enjoy support at court but was immediately attacked by the scholar-antiquary John Leland, and with venom out of all proportion to the relative mildness of his criticism.[12] From then on for the rest of the century, it became virtually obligatory for true believers to take shots at Polydore.

Although the controversy was mainly a sixteenth-century phenomenon, it was by no means unheralded. Some of Geoffrey's own twelfth-century contemporaries had found parts of his history hard to swallow, though they were willing enough to accept it in general. Geoffrey's own effort to establish authentication in a certain "vetustissimus liber" that he had been induced to translate into the British tongue[13] (an effort not uncommon among those who walked the ill-marked line between history and romance) did little to persuade the skeptical. William of Newburgh actually subjected the history to a damaging critique, arguing that it rested on fable and false prophecy rather than on respectable authority and that much of it was inherently preposterous.[14] Nevertheless, Geoffrey's version of the legends, and those that followed, remained invincible until the later Middle Ages. Then that subcurrent of common sense that occasionally bubbles to the surface of English intellectual life in that confused period[15] brought with it a fresh wave of skepticism. John Wethamsted even asserted that for Englishmen to claim nobility from Brutus was "opus vantiatis, et satis ridiculi."[16] Ralph Higden expressed doubts about Arthur. In the *Polychronicon* he noticed, for example, that Geoffrey was the only chronicler who described Arthur as the conqueror of thirty kingdoms, including France and Rome. Higden's translator, John Trevisa, however, took him sharply to task, tried to explain away this and other discrepancies, and listed some of the physical evidence traditionally associated with Arthur—his seal, for example, and the "original" Round Table then hanging on the wall at Winchester.[17] English readers of the later fifteenth century were no doubt ready to accept Sir Thomas Mallory's version of the Arthurian stories as history just as he appears to have done. But sensible old Caxton presented his edition of *Morte Darthur* with a *caveat emptor:* "For to give faith and believe that all is true that is conteyened herein, ye be at your liberty."[18]

By the early sixteenth century, enough skepticism had in fact been engendered about the historicity of the Galfridean tradition in an increasingly humanistic and critical atmosphere to make its future uncertain. Sir Thomas Kendrick may well have been right when he argued that it might not have survived at all had it not been for the outburst of patriotic enthusiasm that followed the advent of the Welsh Tudors, and that, as a result, the British History enjoyed a "reprieve" that lasted for over a century.[19] If, however, it was a reprieve, it was a very uneasy one. The critical atmosphere that had allowed the medieval tradition to be questioned in the preceding centuries continued to exist and, in fact, to intensify. The relative quiet on the part of the critics is belied by the frantic efforts of the "fundamentalists" (as Kendrick aptly called them) to combat Polydore's legacy and by the enormous quantity of ink they spilled relative to that of their opponents. One cannot help surmising that a great deal more informal discussion went on than ever got into print on the anti-Galfridean side.

There are some hints that this was indeed the case. When John Rastell, a member of Thomas More's circle, and a lawyer by profession, took pains in his *Pastime of Pleasure* (published in 1529 before the appearance of Polydore's history) to disprove certain aspects of Geoffrey's story, one might guess that some discussion had taken place within that influential humanist community.[20] A better indication may be found in John Twyne's dialogue *De rebus Albionicis, Britannicis atque Anglicis,* written sometime before the mid-century but not published until 1590. In it, three scholars discuss a number of things pertaining to the early history of the island, including Geoffrey's story of the Trojan origin, and more perceptively withal than anything before Camden's *Brittannia.*[21] In the course of their discussion, the leader pays his personal respects to Vives ("amicus noster").[22] This dialogue surely suggests the possibility that just such a small group actually met in Canterbury. It also points to the probable influence of Vives, whose own critical treatment of contemporary culture could help to account for the demystifying character of Twyne's own treatment of Geoffrey's story.

To follow the controversy over the British History in any detail would be unnecessary, and largely irrelevant anyway, since, for present purposes, it is the fact of belief that is important and the reaction it provided rather than the substance of the arguments. Some aspects of those arguments do, however, cast needed light on the problem of belief.

The battle lines themselves may be drawn for summary purposes with a few strokes: on the one side a profound and stubborn will to believe a story considered an essential part of a cherished national tradition, a will so powerful as to misappropriate the techniques of respectable scholarship and distort its principles; on the other, a scholarship no less patriotic, but sustained more by a desire to get at the truth than by loyalty to an already questioned and questionable legendary history. Both sides shared the desire to rationalize, the same desire that was tending, though much more slowly, to explain the stories of classical mythology in rational terms. But whereas the defenders, especially the Welsh defenders, of the Galfridean tradition sought to make belief reasonable, critics preferred to use rational means to confirm doubts that arose almost as much out of common sense, or a sense of the ridiculous, as out of logic and hard evidence. In pursuit of these aims, both sides used, and often misused, the methods of humanist scholarship. Both also shared a certain fundamental credulity—there was certainly enough of it to go around in a day when the line between truth and fiction was not yet drawn with precision, when people were surrounded daily with things they could not explain rationally, and when God himself was known to move in a mysterious way.

As the supporters of an embattled cause, the defenders of the British History expended more than their share of ammunition. The vast number of books written by them in the course of the sixteenth century is a tribute to the strength, and also to the bitterness, of their feeling. Their opponents, recognizing that time and the weight of evidence was on their side, and well aware of the sensitivity of the issue in a sensitively patriotic society, employed the Fabian tactics of disengagement and simply let the other side defeat itself.

The problem of belief is implicit in the entire controversy. Where little or no hard evidence can be found either to support or reject a legend, it becomes necessary to make the most of hypothesis based on reasoned conjecture. Success, of course, depends on how reasoned the conjecture may be. In the process, however, the historical imagination has to be stretched to the utmost. The more perceptive of Renaissance England's antiquaries and historians, those especially who were exploring the early and less-documented past, recognized this problem of interpretation and knew the importance of conjecture and the uses of probability. Ralegh, as we have seen elsewhere, justified the use of conjecture in estimating second causes provided it did not derogate from the "first cause" and noticed that, in this respect, the historian must "borrow of the poets" whose franchise it was to seek a truth that transcended brute fact. Nor, he added, could the probabilities thus arrived at be considered "feigned."[23] Those who, like Twyne, had to deal with the largely unfounded legends of the British History found it especially important to make use of every scrap of evidence considered legitimate and to fill in the gaps by hypothetical means—to arrive, as Twyne put it (probably reflecting his master, Vives), at whatever bears a "similitude" or likelihood of truth.[24]

Those who took part in the controversy on either side were in fact searching for some basis for belief—or, more accurately, for a degree of understanding that would legitimize their conception of a legendary past for which too little evidence remained for any certainty either of acceptance or rejection. This is true not only of the fundamentalists who supported the British History at all costs, but of those critics whose skepticism was but a means toward a more believable conjecture. Where there was little to go on, skeptics had, like true believers, to complete their search for truth in an act of faith.

John Twyne's effort to demystify the British History is especially instructive, for it illustrates both the potentialities inherent in the humanist approach to the legendary past and its limitations. Twyne realized that successfully to refute the story of Brutus and the Trojan origin of Britain—to expose, that is, the "lies" he believed Geoffrey had injected into the nation's prehistory, he would have to do more than simply point out the weaknesses, nay the absurdities, of that story. In addition, he would have to put something in its place. If the Trojans were not the founders, who were? Using one legend to combat another, as he was only too ready to do, he reconstructed out of very little an Albionic race who, under Albion, the son of Neptune, himself a giant, defeated the giants indigenous to the island and founded a dynasty. But that story explained too little about what subsequently took place, so Twyne was at pains to find a second race of immigrants who became the real founders. The result was his brilliant, if misguided, Phoenician hypothesis. In realizing that Phoenician traders could have, and probably did, reach the British Isles in search of tin, he anticipated that theory by almost a century and may well have started the Phoenicians on their long and mischievous career in English historiography. Further, in an effort to use what little he knew about them in order to account for the characteristics of the society he believed they brought to Britain, he showed his originality once more, as well as the limitations of his imagination, by stretching the methods of humanist philology at times beyond the breaking point, by overly ingenious analyzing of place names, and, more perceptively, by finding parallels between what was known about Phoenician customs and artifacts and those still observable in the England of his own day.[25]

Twyne's capability for imaginative hypothesis and reconstruction shows up also in his startling paleogeographical theory, this time on the right track, that the early migrations could be explained in part by the fact that the island of Britain had once been joined to the mainland by an isthmus which had since been worn away by time and tide. As evidence he pointed to analogous changes in the coastline known to have taken place elsewhere in early times, and in England itself within living memory.[26] Still more perceptive—this time by reading his classical authorities with an unaccustomed realism—was his recognition that the prehistorical peoples of Britain lived not like the well-dressed Trojans ordinarily pictured, but like denizens of a stone age society, naked and painted. If he was influenced here by accounts of American Indians, as he could have been, he did not say so, and it remained for another generation to make that important connection; but he appears to have been the first English writer to make the fully as important connection between the barbarism he believed exemplified by his own island ancestors and that of all primitive peoples as they were coming to be envisioned in the age-old "cave myth," then enjoying a considerable revival.[27]

It was Camden, however, who said the last word in the Tudor period for the critics of the Trojan legend, albeit with perhaps excessive politeness. A man of vast erudition and well connected with Continental scholarship, he was better able than the Canterbury schoolmaster to see the prehistoric world steadily and see it whole. Despite his own considerable learning and humanist connections, Twyne was, after all, more remarkable for his imaginative insights than for the weight of his scholarship. Still, Camden could have been more forthright in his criticism of the medieval tradition. He was more interested in the antiquities of those ages for which he had hard evidence, Roman Britain, for example, than in those that, he said, "abide in great darkness, error and ignorance."[28] But he could hardly ignore the vexing problem of the earliest inhabitants. As was customary in such projects, he had to begin his monumental chorographical work, *Britannia,* at the very beginning, which meant dealing at once with the problem of Geoffrey and his tradition. He accordingly summed up the opinion against it so effectively as to make the arguments of the conservatives appear as futile as they really were. But he did so with caution and the appearance of a neutral observer issuing a friendly caveat.

If there is any doubt that the British History had become a patriotic religion which it was still, in the late sixteenth century, heretical to criticize, one has only to read Camden's careful disclaimers. He had, he said, no intention of discrediting Geoffrey, for to do so would be "to strive with the stream and current of Time; and to struggle against an opinion commonly and long since received." So he would "let every man . . . judge as it pleaseth him." Moreover, legends similar to the Trojan were not uncommon: they could be found among the French, Scots, Irish, Danes, Goths, and Saxons. Citing Varro, he went so far as to suggest that it is profitable for a people to believe, "although untimely," that they are descended from gods.[29]

Not that Camden himself suffered from serious doubts. The question of the earliest inhabitants, he noted, was moot, in any case, due to lack of records for the "fabulous" period before the first Olympiad. The first Latin writer he knew of even to mention Britain was Lucretius, and he lived "but little before Caesar."[30] As for the early inhabitants themselves, they "had other cases and thoughts to busy and trouble their heads than to deliver their beginnings to posterity."[31] The Druids, who alone "sang noble and valourous acts," did not believe in writing books, and later generations simply made up for the resulting deficiency by inventing stories. Camden was nevertheless able to marshal an array of learned opinion—ancient, medieval and contemporary, foreign and domestic—against the Trojan legend so formidable as to convince all but the truest of believers.

Moreover, Camden, like Twyne, had a theory about who to put in place of the Trojans. Here he, too, resorted to hypothesis based on scholarly conjecture. It was the Gauls, he argued, the descendants of Gomer, Noah's eldest son, who had not only established themselves in France and Germany but had probably reached Britain. The Britons were, therefore, in all probability, "the offspring of Gauls." This proposition he backed up by a wealth of sophisticated argument based on similarities of customs, language, and artifacts—but especially language, "the surest proof of peoples' original."[32]

The defenders of the fundamentalist orthodoxy faced, in some respects, a more difficult and complex task. As they no doubt feared, the opposition was surely more pervasive than the relatively small number of books they wrote would indicate, and it was deeply entrenched in the more liberal segment of the learned community. As a result, the conservatives felt driven to rely on questionable evidence and to develop overly subtle and overly imaginative arguments. While present-day scholars understandably find appealing the skepticism, the good sense, and the respect for evidence shown by those who sought to demystify the national history, they should be careful not to underestimate the scholarship of its opponents. In some respects, Leland showed more originality in his defense of Geoffrey than did Polydore in his criticism of him.[33] Whereas Polydore, like critics before him, rested his case mainly on the silence of the Roman writers, Leland at least sought such positive evidence, however questionable much of it may have been, as his chorographical survey of actual sites might provide. Critics in fact continued, up to Camden himself, to rely to a large extent on classical authority. Sir John Price, certainly the most scholarly of the spokesmen for the conservative cause, would, left to himself, have cut a distinguished figure as an historian-antiquary. His son noted, in the dedicatory epistle he wrote for his *Historiae Britannicae defensio* (1573, but written a quarter century earlier), that Price's scholarship exemplified the criteria that Jean Bodin prescribed for anyone who would explore the early history of any people: knowledge of their history, of their language, and of the region's historical sites. If one allows for a certain amount of filial piety, this is a fair enough estimate of what was at least Price's potential.

Price advanced a number of sensible arguments as well as many highly imaginary ones. For example, against the point that the respected Roman authors made no mention of Brutus and his Trojans, he argued that they were, after all, chroniclers of their own people and could not have been expected to know or care much about the early history of remote Britain, and he added that, if Tacitus could do no better than he did with so important a history as that of the Jews, how much better would he and his sort be expected to have done in the more peripheral case of the Britons?[34]

Like his fellow Welsh patriot Humphrey Lhuyd, Price pointed to a real, if largely theoretical, weakness in the scholarship of their opponents, namely their lack of knowledge of the early British language.[35] He was quick to realize that this emphasis on the importance of the British language would help him get around the opposition's point that no written evidence had come down from early British times. The Britons, he maintained, had indeed cultivated a strong oral tradition and possessed, in the Druids, a succession of trained historians, and it therefore did not matter that their work did not find written expression until a later time. He pointed out, moreover, that oral tradition could have been, and was, passed on by prophetic singers called bards, poets, or "vates," men such as Taliesin and Merlin, whose professional function was to celebrate heroes. Some of their songs have, he said, come down to the present day and are available to anyone who can understand the British tongue, a fact which, Price proudly asserts, could hardly be said of any other language—witness the "Anglica lingua" that in books over three hundred years old can scarcely be understood at all.[36] This, then, the literary condensation of oral tradition, constituted the evidence critics unversed in the British language had persistently overlooked.

This is all well and good, in intent if not in substance. Price's recognition of the potential inherent in oral tradition was unusually perceptive; and, considered as a hypothesis, his idea that a historical record was passed on from early times to bards whose songs came eventually to be written down is not bad, as hypothetical thinking went in those days. But neither he nor his colleagues on the right could stay long within range of reasonable conjecture. Despite his resort to oral tradition, Price was able, for example, to convince himself that the ancient Britons had letters "ab initio," and that there was no time when men of letters or education in the liberal arts could not be found among them—the means, in other words, by which they could preserve their history.[37] This preoccupation with language, typical though it was of the humanist philological method, led these defenders of the British History to guesswork far beyond what was common enough among respectable scholars.

Humphrey Lhuyd, an otherwise capable scholar, went still further, maintaining that anyone "exercised in the reading of Histories" knows that "Philosophy and the liberal sciences were known to the Celtae and Britons before they were known to the Greeks and Latins."[38] Convinced, as were his fellows, that the history of the earliest times and the fluid relationship that existed between peoples in the postdiluvian world could best be traced by way of linguistic similarities, he took that familiar principle as license to make the most imaginative comparisons between Celtic words and those in Hebrew, Greek, and Latin, to say nothing of contemporary German and Spanish, and even, though with commendable hesitancy, "Mexicani."[39]

It would be hard to exaggerate the lengths to which minds of this period would go in the interests of preserving a cherished historical belief, or of denouncing a hated heresy. Not that the critics of the Galfridean tradition were innocent in this respect. But the most scholarly of the defenders tended to lose all perspective when their patriotic sensibilities were involved. With the increasing undercurrent of skepticism that flows from the later medieval period itself and the new sense of history supposed to derive from humanism, it is not easy, as Kendrick has said, "to understand the muddle-headed deliberateness with which antiquaries of acknowledged learning continued to adorn the already fantastic British History with tatters and scraps of an even more nonsensical and irresponsible guesswork."[40]

The defenders of the British History were actually more interested in King Arthur than in Brutus. This is not surprising considering the Welsh perspective shared by many of them. But the appeal of Arthur transcended Welsh patriotism. Arthur was, after all, the outstanding figure in Geoffrey's story. Despite its brilliance, the account Geoffrey gave of Brutus and his exploits is no match for the tales of Arthur and his knights, still less for the Arthur whose reputation had been enhanced by the Arthurian romances relayed to English readers by Sir Thomas Mallory. Arthur was better able than the more distant Brutus to symbolize the Tudor monarchy. More even than the chivalric Arthur, whose image shone again for a while during the Elizabethan revival of chivalry, it was Arthur the national hero and conqueror who seized the patriotic imagination of English readers. Indeed it was Arthur rather than Brutus who really precipitated the outburst of opposition to Polydore Vergil. Nevertheless, the Arthurians could not avoid involvement in the Brutus controversy. They realized that the British History was indivisible: if Brutus were to lose his historical credentials, the whole tradition would be in trouble, Arthur included. So the Arthurian material was of primary strategic importance to the true believers, just as Brutus remained strategically essential to the critics.[41] It also accounts for more than its share of the bitterness that made the Arthurians at times sound, in the unbridled vituperation of their attack on Polydore—and all things Roman for that matter—like the contestants in the confessional controversies of that Reformation era.[42]

The Arthurians could be very persuasive, nor, according to the standards of the day, did their points always lack substance. They were able to counter the arguments made by the critics based on the silence of the ancient authors—and especially on that of Gildas, the British author who, if anyone, should have mentioned Arthur—by showing, as Price did for the Brutus legend, that none of those authorities could have been expected to know about Arthur or feel called upon to mention him. But they succeeded especially in marshaling the more tangible evidence for Arthur's existence, and with it to outflank the argument from authority. As Price did with Celtic bards, Leland did with what then passed for archeological evidence. "I betake me," he wrote, "unto the Rocks and monuments, the true witnesses of Arthur's renown and magesty."[43] This faith in the pioneering chorographic investigations he was undertaking may seem excessive: there was still much in him of "the scholastic chronicler-antiquary who is content to repeat a satisfying fable without disturbing inquiry into its probability."[44] He was able, nevertheless, to collect what he believed to be convincing evidence of Arthur's existence. He had seen, for example, Arthur's tomb and the leaden cross taken from it bearing Arthur's name, Arthur's great seal in Westminster Abbey, and the Round Table itself, hanging in Winchester. He had also noticed what he believed to be the clearly Arthurian character of innumerable place names which, if not immediately evident, could be made plain by the manipulation of a philological learning more ingenious than sound.[45]

Much of this information had, of course, been in circulation for a long time and was widely accepted as genuine. That much of it was spurious, and was coming in some quarters to be regarded as such, did not decrease its believability in the eyes of those bent on believing. Yet critics had little trouble dealing with it. John Rastell, for example, effectively questioned the authenticity of Arthur's seal.[46] And Camden, not surprisingly, refused to accept as genuine the Round Table at Winchester, "which the common sort useth to gaze upon with great admiration, as if it had been Arthur's table."[47]

There was a point, however, beyond which even true believers could not go. Leland, himself, readily admitted that the authors who had propagated Arthur's story had allowed "lies" (i.e., fiction) to creep into it, but insisted that such "obscure and absurd reports" should not detract from the truth which otherwise rested on good authority.[48] Where the Arthurians would draw the line between truth and fiction remained, however, unclear. If the readers of the poetic histories written by William Warner and Michael Drayton[49] were taken at face value, almost unlimited belief in the entire

British History might be thought to exist in the minds of Elizabethan and Jacobean readers. Yet Drayton asked Selden to write commentaries on the text of his *Poly-Olbion* presumably to create some balance between fact and poetic history or (it often meant the same thing) fiction.[50] Certainly Selden was as forthright in his criticism of the Arthurian material as he thought it prudent to be, considering his youth at the time and the common will to believe a still cherished story. He complained that some "too hyperbolic stories have made him a larger conqueror on every adjacent country, as the Muse [Drayton] recites," and that the "bard's songs have, with this kind of unlimited attribute so laden him, that you can hardly guess what is true of him." Arthur, he adds, should be remembered "as a man right worthy to have been celebrated by true story, not false tales."[51] This estimate pretty well sums up the attitude of those who criticized the British History as well as of most moderate believers—even Price refused to accept the stories of Arthur's campaigns and battles "aliunde confictas et adiectas"[52]—though it is worth noticing that Dr. John Dee, Elizabeth's brilliant and eccentric magus, would still maintain that the account of Arthur's foreign conquests supported the rights of the English crown to Ireland and a North Sea empire.[53]

The Arthur that was emerging from the dust and smoke of the British History controversy was for the most part a figure that, from the historical point of view, had been cut down to human proportions—"a notable and valorous and religious prince," as John Harrington called him,[54] and little more; yet as a symbolic figure he continued to inspire pageantry and poetry. One did not have to believe in the total Arthur of the British History, or, for that matter in the British History, to use both for their symbolic value, as Spenser did in *The Faerie Queene*. Nor did the skepticism that tinged the atmosphere of early seventeenth-century intellectual life prevent James I from using the prestige of Arthur to bolster his own. While the Arthurian legend, unlike that of Brutus, remained very much alive, it was rapidly moving beyond the point where the question of its historicity retained any relevance.

Brutus and the Trojans did not, in fact, fare so well as Arthur and his knights. Never the equal of Arthur as a source of inspiration, Brutus lacked the kind of appeal that was to make possible periodic revivals of Arthurian romanticism. Once his claim to historicity had faded, his story had little but the thinnest of antiquarianism going for it. Yet his virtual disappearance from the main historical scene had less to do with the success of the critics of the British History in outlasting the defenders than with the fact that a new breed of antiquaries, typified by the Elizabethan Society of Antiquaries formed about 1580, was shifting the direction of interest.[55] The revival of Saxon studies in the later Elizabethan decades had given these practical-minded gentlemen-scholars something they could really handle, that they could document, in place of the largely fictional history that had sprung from Geoffrey of Monmouth's fertile brain.

Except where it enjoyed continued support as, more or less admittedly, the stuff of poetic history, the Trojan legend appears to have suffered a steady erosion of belief. In 1529, John Rastell had noted that there were some men "today" who "take that story of Galfridus but for a feigned fable" concocted to glorify his Welsh heritage.[56] Roughly a century later, John Selden commented that to "reckon the learned men who deny him [Brutus] . . . were too long a catalogue."[57] Whatever may have been the popular will to believe, the learned world by then had begun, as Kendrick put it, "to delight in incredulity and doubt."[58]

By then, too, Camden had committed himself to "rejecting all fabulous fictions" contained in the monuments of antiquity[59] and had subjected the Trojan legend to an examination so judicious as to leave little for his successors to do. Though more sympathetic to medieval culture than most of those who shared his humanist background, Samuel Daniel declared bluntly that the legend was the work of "Ignorance and Credulity."[60] His fellow historian John Clapham noticed that "divers writers hold it suspected, reputing it (for good reason) rather a Poetical Fiction, than a true History," and called for a critical review of the tradition on which the Tudor chroniclers had depended for their earliest history in the interests of "things, either truly done, or at least warranted by probability."[61]

Yet we must not exaggerate the extent of this apparent victory of skepticism over belief. Like their neighbors, the English still needed a beginning. Without being able to go back confidently to origins, without finding a vanishing point for their historical perspective, they felt a sense of intellectual insecurity. Nor were they entirely happy with a distant past they knew to be largely imaginary. That is why so many of them preferred to cling to their legends in the face of compelling criticism of their historicity. The resulting internal conflict, moreover, was by no means confined to the world of antiquarian scholarship. Lawyers, for example, with their preoccupation with precedent and the myth they nourished that the common law itself was of immemorial antiquity, not surprisingly found themselves resorting to the British History. Sir Edward Coke, the greatest legal mind of Jacobean England, could speak more than half seriously of a law book written by Brutus, though he admitted that he would not "examine those things in *quo qarranto*."[62] His contemporary George Salter, however, wrote a legal treatise in which he accepted the legendary history with no reservations at all.[63]

Even when they abandoned the legendary history, many did so with admitted reluctance. A lingering wish to believe, if only it were possible, tended to temper the skepticism of even the more confirmed unbelievers. This wish to believe was kept alive by the suspicion that, if only more were known about the legendary past, more might be believed. Even Camden ("solid Camden" a contemporary called him) cautioned his readers to remember that some things that at first look false may "on better review" appear true.[64] Though Selden refused to take any responsibility for the historicity of Drayton's version of the British History, he called attention to the loss of trustworthy evidence that, he could not help thinking, might otherwise have verified stories now considered fabulous. Speaking of the Arthurian legends in particular, he pointed to the well-known fact that the nation's written records had suffered from wave after wave of despoilers,[65] and suggested that oral tradition would have been more trustworthy had the practice of periodic peer trial, to which early British minstrels were subjected, been maintained.[66] As it was, he could only lament that "this critic age" would no longer believe the stories about the nation's founders "because of their unlikely and fictitious mixtures."[67] There remained also the nagging suspicion that a kernel of truth might remain within all legends, no matter how fabulous they might seem. Spenser, who had no use for the Brutus story, had to admit that "under the tales ye may in a measure see the truth lurk."[68] Many years later we find John Milton likewise clinging to the wreckage of the British History: despite its exclusion by "judicious Antiquaries," the Brutus legend contained, if not truth, at least the "footprints of something true," and so retained matter legitimately useful to poets and rhetoricians.[69]

The controversy over the British History not only called attention as never before to problems involved in dealing with the historicity of a legendary prehistory, but also afforded its participants an unparalleled opportunity to see the mythopoeic process itself in historical perspective, and, in particular, to examine the role of poets and, though more tentatively, that of oral tradition, within it. All agreed that the legends had been passed on initially by Celtic bards, but the two sides disagreed over the trustworthiness of bardic tradition. Price tried to establish the cultural credentials of such famous bards as Taliesin and Merlin by arguing that they had enjoyed much the same educational benefits as those of much later ages, including schools specifically devoted to teaching how to make songs that memorialize heroes.[70] Critics, on the other hand, stressed the degree to which "unlettered bards" had developed the stories so imaginatively as to render them virtually useless as history.[71] As the reader may recall, Selden charged that "bardic impostures" had made the British legends no more historical than the stories told by Ariosto, Rabelais, or Spenser.[72] It is also worth remembering that Spenser himself had had experience with an analogous problem involved in the bardic legends of Ireland, and had worked out a relatively sophisticated methodology for sifting fact from fancy and for arriving at a believable history of Irish society.[73]

The similarity between the role of the Celtic bards and that of the ancient poets could hardly have escaped the notice of participants in the controversy over the legacy of Geoffrey. Twyne recognized the parallel between Geoffrey and Homer, albeit as "liars."[74] Drayton made a similar comparison, though for the opposite reason: the songs of Taliesin, he insisted, were not "idle tales" nor "fabulous, like those devised by the Greeks."[75] It was becoming ever clearer that the role of poets in the transmission of legends and the making of myths was universal. William Harrison, for example, noticed in his historical description of England that something very like the tendency of Celtic bards to move away from an original priestly function only to become spinners of fabulous tales about valiant princes had also been observed in "New Spain."[76] And Price, though a true believer, was able to see that the creation of legends was a process through which all peoples had passed. From the very beginning, he wrote, they had all taken pains to memorialize the deeds done by their ancestors in both symbol and legend: "Hence the use of hieroglyphics before the discovery of letters, hence the fables of poets."[77]

The controversy within the microcosmic world of British legend unquestionably helped bring the problem of history-in-myth into clearer focus. How far the experience gained in the course of it carried over into the macrocosm of classical mythology is another question, an interesting one but one not easy to answer. The evidence is admittedly slender. The issue was not in itself a matter of debate. Yet there is reason to believe that a significant minority of English writers of humanist background recognized a generic relationship between the mythology of classical antiquity and the legendary history of British antiquity. Camden considered both characteristic of that period in the evolution of historical consciousness that Varro had termed "fabulous."[78] Then there was the analogy, too obvious to escape notice, between the heroes of the British legends and the gods and heroes of classical myth. Polydore Vergil had seen nothing suprising in England's love affair with Geoffrey: most peoples, he pointed out, derived their origins from the gods and, like the Romans, believed their histories, no matter how fabulous they might be.[79] Twyne had come to much the same conclusion in his more extensive examination of the Trojan myth. A people, he concluded, will believe whatever it wants to, and he saw that there will always be those who are ready to reshape the legendary past in order to give mythic enhancement to the present.[80] The tendency of Welsh patriots of his own day to arrogate to themselves the history of Troy and the prophecy of *Arthurus redivivus,* was not, Twyne said, unlike the tendency of the ancients to make gods and demigods of their heroes.[81] Selden provided an oddly appropriate example. Among his annotations to Drayton's *Poly-Olbion,* he made a passing reference that suggests he, too, had come to realize that Arthurian legends had developed into a myth comparable to the myths of antiquity. Skeptically contemplating the story involving Uther's lust for Igerne, wife of Golois, Prince of Cornwall, their marriage after the latter's death, and the subsequent birth of Arthur, he noticed that "here you have a Jupiter, an Alcmena, and Amphitryo, a Saphias, and a Mercury; nor want there scarce any thing, but that truth-passing reports of Poetical bards have made the birth an Hercules."[82]

Having seen the reaction of Tudor and early Stuart English minds to the British legends, we are left, as in the case of the classical myth-history, with questions not answerable with any finality. One may presume sincerity of belief in those who so vigorously and with such emotional intensity defended the medieval tradition. One cannot be so sure about the quality of skepticism displayed by the critics of it. The fact is that, though the study of man had progressed to the point where it was able to foster a perspective of doubt, it had not as yet reached the point where skepticism could develop into confident disbelief. Even the most skeptical had still to cope with the suspicion that if only more were known of the legendary past, more of it might be believed, and the conviction that a kernel of truth must "lurk," to use Spenser's word, in all legends, however fabulous they may be.

From the average English reader's point of view, however, it probably did not really matter whether the legends were true or not. For him it was what they meant that mattered. Together they still served as a living mythology. Unlike the classical myths that influenced Renaissance thought deeply, but by way of symbol and allegory, and therefore ahistorically, the British History, whether or not it was accorded literal belief, appealed directly to a people finding its way through a period of confusing change and therefore much in need of the kind of self-image that depended on historical perspective—one, moreover, that extended historical vision into utter antiquity. Although Brutus failed to survive in the popular memory, the legend of Troy continued to reappear in pageantry and poetry, and helped, as to a still greater extent did the Arthurian legends, to focus Tudor national feeling. Arthur's knights provided the stuff essential to the Elizabethan revival of chivalry, as, indeed, they and their king continued to do for the later revival of Victoria's reign.

Some clues to the twin problems of skepticism and belief may nevertheless be found in the contemporaneous discussion of the relation of history to poetry and, more particularly, of "poesie historical" as an interpretive device. A later chapter will be devoted to this epistemological problem.

6

A Digression on Giants

Among the flights of historical fancy that swirled around the problem of Britain's beginnings, giants constituted a minor but persistent theme, and one that deserves examination because it exemplifies, in its way, the same conflict between the will to believe and the slowly gathering doubts as did the major controversy. Although the debate over the British History turned largely on the Trojan legend, it could not help raising the ultimate question, Who were actually the earliest inhabitants? Certainly the Trojans could not have been: the Trojan War was a relatively late event, after all. And anyway, Geoffrey had stated clearly that Brutus and his Trojan followers encountered a race of giants on their arrival at the island. The notion of indigenous giants was also perpetuated, even by otherwise respectable historiographers, by that preposterous tale about the part played in propagating the race of giants by those terrible daughters of Danaus who somehow found their way across the seas to Britain and there cohabited with giants.[1]

Giants figured in still another line of legend, one that enjoyed for a while a degree of support that rivaled that afforded Galfridian orthodoxy. It stemmed, as we have seen in the preceding chapter, from the forgery by Annius of Viterbo purporting to be the work of Berosus, the ancient Chaldean sage. As domesticated in England by John Bale, this story told of a certain Samothes, son of Japhet and grandson of Noah himself, and, according to Annius, a giant in his own right, who, in the course of the repopulation of the world after the Flood, became ruler of the Britons and Gauls centuries before the arrival of the Trojans in Britain.[2] Meanwhile, so the story goes, a collateral line had come down from Ham, Noah's "evil" son, through Osiris and Neptune to Albion, the wicked giant who inaugurated a sort of iron age in British history. This legend prompted not only Bale but the usually more level-headed humanist John Twyne to propose a pre-Trojan Albionic civilization.

The historical problem posed by giants had, of course, a life of its own to which the English controversy was only incidental, a history as old as antiquity itself.[3] Giants had, from the beginning, figured in the pseudo-history of the ancient mythologies, and they continued to live and prosper not only in folklore but in the writings of the erudite. Although, as archetypes, they often served the ends of allegory and symbol, sometimes in the pursuit of political propaganda, such usages were by no means incompatible with a belief in their historicity. No one was in any case likely to challenge the authority of Genesis 6:4. There were, indeed, giants in those days. The only serious historical question remaining was how the giants of the Old Testament managed to survive the Flood. But that question proved really irrelevant because giants remained far too deeply engaged in popular imaginings and erudite tradition, too useful, in fact, to be so easily disposed of. Once again they proved useful to those Renaissance authors who repeated the legends that told of the nation's eponymous heroes—now usually conceived as good giants in the Herculean mold, rather than the traditional monsters more frequently met with in stories and whom they, too, had on occasion to encounter.

Although giants kept a relatively low profile in the British History and the problem of their historicity did not, per se, play a large part in the controversy over it, the very fact that they were involved at all gave special point to such misgivings about them as were likely to surface anyway in a society increasingly given to demanding explanations that would accord with reason and experience. English intellectuals, however, were not yet ready to give up their giants—Ralegh, for example, was as ready as Higden, his medieval counterpart as a universal historian, to believe that giants existed in history[4]—but they preferred to rationalize them as far as possible within the context of history rather than to question their right to be there.

In the course of the discussion of England's prehistory, the interlocutors of Twyne's dialogue *De rebus Albionicis, Britannicis atque Anglicis*[5] had reason to give at least passing thought to the part played in it by giants. The two younger scholars who had met with the elderly Abbot Foch seem, indeed, to have had giants on their minds. They keep asking not only about the legends concerning giants as the earliest inhabitants, but about the historical reality of giants in general. The abbot, presumably speaking for the author, appears less interested, preferring to talk about the Albionic regime and about his favorite Phoenicians, who he thought more likely to have actually colonized Britain than the Trojans.[6] But before they decide to leave the topic, they have managed to touch upon most of its vital parts. The group agrees that there were giants in those days. They cite, of course, the standard classical and biblical sources. But they seem especially reassured by such empirical evidence as they thought provided by the unnaturally large bones known to have been exhumed at one time or another, even within living memory, and by the monolithic remains widely observable throughout England, Stonehenge being only the most famous, which must surely have been the work of giants. Such evidence, they believe, gives the lie to "the opinion of many" that giants are merely the figment of the poetic imagination, calculated to terrify women and children.[7]

Pressed for a pronouncement, the good abbot proceeds to analyze the giants' place in history—or rather in that part of the pseudo-history of myth and legend that he is prepared to accept as history—under four categories.[8] First, there are those personages who have figured in most legends of origin as founders and heroes—Gomer for the Germans and Gauls, for example, and Tubal for the Spaniards, and Albion for the English—and who came to be called giants simply by virtue of their priority in time and their signal service. Second, there are those who, in the days before the decline of the human race in size and vigor, were noted for unusual physical size, men such as Goliath of the Old Testament and certain peoples of Africa reported upon by Pliny. Giants of this sort have left traces still visible in England, such as "mounds, fortifications, caves, monuments of stone, giants' dances, and tombs."[9] Third, there are those various characters mentioned in both classical and biblical literature who earned their designation as "giants and cyclopses" because of their cruelty, tyranny, and impiety. Fourth and last, there are the good giants, those who tended to be called giants as it were by courtesy (*ex dignitate*) for their beneficent services. Such were Atlas, Orpheus, and Hercules.

Twyne tried to demystify the traditional giants just as he tried to demystify the whole of England's prehistory. He sought not only to avoid the patently fabulous but also to draw giants into the context of history. His account of the elevation of great, but otherwise presumably normal men, heroes of one sort or another, to the status of giants suggests to us, as it no doubt did to him, a process similar to the euhemeristic deification of mortals. Also, by linking England's aboriginal giants with the cave dwellers who, according to classical tradition, represented mankind's earliest state, he brought both within the context of the "cave myth" that for so many Renaissance minds served as a focal point for historical speculation.[10] Both apparently shared the utterly exigent life considered, according to that tradition, generally characteristic of primitive man: "Haec vita primorum parentum fuit."[11]

Despite his effort to historicize giants—perhaps indeed because, in his zeal to rationalize, he protested too much—Twyne reveals the ambivalence that was to mark attitudes toward the problem of giants for the ensuing century, just as it was to mark attitudes toward the mythological pseudo-history.[12] English intellectuals were too committed to the primacy of reason in regard to things human and to the evidence of experience to accept the traditional stories about giants entirely at face value, yet those who were concerned enough to comment at all still felt the need to rationalize their appearance in myth and legend. Some even went to curious lengths to do so. One respected writer of the late Elizabethan years even hinted that the giants the Trojans encountered on their arrival might have been the result of spontaneous generation from the earth itself. Although he took a neutral position between this Lucretian myth and the orthodox Adamic story, he reflects the dilemma then facing minds torn between monogenetic theories and the possibilities inherent in polygenetic alternatives.[13]

A similar ambivalence marks the effort of Alexander Ross to give the legendary giants their proper place in the traditional mythology. In his own curious mythologia entitled *Mystagogus Poeticus* (1648), he combined the common will to rationalize with his own compulsive desire to give allegorical significance to the traditional myths, including those that involved giants. While hastening to show how giants have been given such purely symbolic roles as "notorious and profane men," rebels against authority, and deniers of Christ's divinity, and how they could in ancient mythology even personify "winds and vapors," he also treats them historically and naturalistically: "That there were men of an huge stature, fierce looks, and of wicked disposition, and of high and proud minds . . . is not to be doubted," as witness not only Scripture but the recent testimony of Scaliger who actually saw one in Italy so tall he could not stand but had to lie on two beds joined in length. "All ages," he maintained, "have produced some such giants," but he will have none of the notion that they were begot of devils and women; for, he pointed out, with an argument so ingeniously rational as to reduce the problem to a new level of absurdity, such a union would have been clearly against nature: since spirits and people are of different species, their offspring could only have been hybrids and hence, like mules, sterile! No, "these giants were men, not different from other men, either in their matter or form, but only in greatness."[14]

Meanwhile, however, a work had arrived in England that injected an unsettling shot of raw rationalism into the discussion. In his *Gigantomachia* (1569),[15] the Antwerpian scholar Goropius argued that giants never really existed and that the term "giant" had originally been applied to oppressors, and only because of their oppression, not because of preternatural stature. This latter point was, of course, hardly original—in three of Twyne's four categories, giants owed their historical status to their actions rather than to their size—but it was gaining strength. It was receiving some support from the several commentators on Genesis who tended, wherever possible, to rationalize the whole of its story.[16] Goropius nevertheless put the more conservative scholars of England on the defensive. Both Ralegh and Harrison took special and sharp issue with "the Antwerpian." Harrison, in fact, devoted an entire chapter of his *Historical Description of the Island of Britain* to this effort to "confute Goropius, and all his cavillations."[17]

Although worried lest reports of giants inhabiting "our island" might cause some people to "suspect the credit of our whole history, and reject it as a fable," Harrison was not so much concerned with Britain's aboriginal giants as he was with the historical reality of giants in general. They were, after all, indigenous inhabitants in his pictured world. While taking for granted the authority of "learned divines," as well as that of the familiar pagan authors, he based his confidence primarily on what one might call the natural history of giants, especially the familiar reports of gigantic bones—"some of late years," some he had seen himself—this despite the opinion of Goropius that they were more likely the remains of an elephant. Like many other apologists for giants, Harrison pressed into his service the still pervasive myth of nature's decay. Though he notes that Goropius sought to prove that people had been much the same at all times by comparing ancient and contemporary methods of measuring, Harrison found the contrary borne out by the "fact" that the bodies of King Arthur and William the Conqueror were one to two feet longer than those of living men: "Wherefore it appeareth by present experience, that all is not absolutely untrue which is remembered of such giants," and "the opinion of giants is not altogether grounded upon vane and fabulous narrations, invented to delight the ears of hearers with the report of marvellous things."[18]

Despite the will to believe that so clearly prompted Harrison's approach, the odor of doubt rises faintly but perceptibly even from these brave words. Nor is this surprising. Here, as in the parallel cases of biblical and classical pseudo-history, naturalistic explanations had become habitual for all who sought to balance reason and belief. But, as in those other respects too, efforts to historicize by such explanations were likely to prove self-defeating, and in late Elizabethan and Jacobean England there were some who had become skeptical to the point of disbelief. Forced in his early years by his editorial duties in relation to Drayton's *Poly-Olbion* to pass some historical judgment on the legend of Britain's aboriginal giants, John Selden was as skeptical as tact would then allow. He had, he acknowledged, read about giants in Holy Writ and the classics, but he could not help feeling that "nature (now as fertile as of old) hath in his effects determinate limits of quantity" and that, to judge from the beds of people in Aristotle's time which were "but six foot ordinarily," men were then about the same size as they are now, and that giants were simply men "of more than vulgar excellence in body and martial performance." (It is worth noting how closely the belief in the legends of giants was involved in the seventeenth-century controversy over the supposed decay of the world.) As for reports of "great bones," Selden, like Goropius, thought they were probably those of large beasts, perhaps even the elephants Claudius was reputed to have brought to Britain to intimidate the natives; for "the eye's judgment in such like hath been, and is, subject to much imposture."[19] Selden chose also to be skeptical about the tradition that explained Stonehenge as initially the work of giants who brought the stones ("chorea gigantium") to Ireland whence they were brought to England by the help of Merlin's spells.[20] If the young Selden was here being overly cautious in the presence of time-honored tradition, his contemporary Inigo Jones, in his mature years, felt no such restraint, and in his treatise on Stonehenge, gave short shrift to the notion.[21]

Skepticism was quite evidently eroding belief in the historical existence of giants, but to the modern mind, accustomed to encountering giants only in romance or in nursery tales, the slowness of the process may seem surprising, especially in view of the appeal to reason and experience that had become apparent in the controversy over the British History. But it should not be so surprising. Renaissance minds were, after all, accustomed to marvels, and enjoyed them. And for those, less numerous, who were becoming wary of them and preferred the evidence of experience, there were always those seemingly convincing grave remains. Moreover, such intellectuals as were willing enough to challenge the traditions embodied in folklore, and may even have nourished suspicions about the evidence of graves, were much less willing to challenge the authority of Scripture. So, in the controversy over the British History, contestants found it easier to slide over the giants in the story and to concentrate on the more relevant human element.

Much the same conditions continued to affect acceptance of historical giants during the remainder of the seventeenth century, albeit to a decreasing extent. The Baconian tradition, with its emphasis on empirical evidence, was unquestionably creating a climate unfavorable to belief in giants. Thomas Molyneux probably expressed the attitude of the more open-minded of his colleagues in that bastion of Baconianism, the Royal Society, when, at the turn of the century, he pointed to the paucity of evidence to support ancient accounts of giants. "Till some such evidence be produced," he remarked, "we may look upon all the stories of those extravagantly Gigantish men, to be little better than the Fables of the Poets of old, or the Whims and Romances of some modern Credulous and Inventive men."[22] This cautious disclaimer, however, amounted to little more than the feeling we have observed among the skeptics in the British History controversy, that if more were known about the legendary past, more might be believable. In any case, the authority of the Pentateuch remained a major obstacle to any such free thinking, and it is no doubt largely for that reason that giants continued to figure in the thinking of antiquaries well into the following century.[23]

7

"Poesie Historical"

One thing the controversy over British origins had contributed to an understanding of the mythic past was the opportunity for examining at relatively close range the role of poets in the mythmaking process and, incidentally, for giving some thought to the relation of poetry to history. It had done other, and important things, too. It had shown how effective the newer tools of historical and textual criticism, even those of a nascent archaeology, could be in demystifying the legendary past and to that extent clarifying whatever truth remained in the legends. But it had also shown the point beyond which such methods could not go in dealing with prehistory. Beyond that point, the most distant past simply refused to be demystified. From then on, the questioner was on his own, the only tool left to him being the historical imagination, and his only witnesses the "poets." As he moved from the middle distance of national legend to the ultimate distance of the age of myth, the problem became still more difficult. He had to deal with the ancient poets as mythmakers and with their relation to history in its most rarified form. Perceptions of prehistory thus came inevitably to be involved with the then controversial problem of poetic truth as it related to history. If there was such a thing as a philosophy of prehistory, it evolved within the parameters of literary criticism.

To modern eyes, the distinction between fact and fiction appears obvious, whether the "hard" fact of empirical scholarship is meant or the extended truth recovered by means of interpretation. It was by no means so obvious to Renaissance minds, to those especially who found themselves, whether they set out to do so or not, grappling with problems involved in the relationship between imaginative literature and a prehistory shrouded in myth and legend.

Nor was their intellectual heritage much help. The classical authors to whom they looked for inspiration offered but a divided counsel, more likely to foster confusion and ambivalence than guidance. Plato held so low an opinion of poets' ability to express truth that he banished them from his ideal state, and he criticized, in particular, the treatment of the gods in Homer and Hesiod.[1] His criticism rests on moral rather than historical grounds. And his generation was just beginning to be aware that religion itself had a history, yet it could see no farther than the early poets.[2] Euhemerists brought the gods into a specifically historical context by recognizing the role of poets in their apotheosis. But classical authors seem, in general, not to have been especially exercised over truth about the past, or about the poet's responsibility for it.[3] They might criticize Homer and the rest for adulterating a true story, for mixing history and myth, yet they tended for the most part to justify imaginative treatment. Cicero, indeed, treated the problem of historical truth itself primarily as one involving rhetorical expression. *Historia,* defined as an account of things done in the distant past, he classified as a species of the genus *narratio,* along with *fabula,* that which is neither true nor verisimilar, and *argumentum,* a fictional story that is nevertheless true to life.[4] Aristotle's *Poetics* did, it is true, provide authors of Tudor England with a positive basis for discussion of the relation of poetry to history. It helped, in particular, to legitimize the shadowy area of "probable truth," where, if anywhere, the notion of "poesie historical" could claim legal residence.[5]

The Hebrew tradition, on the other hand, tended to draw a deceptively sharp line between a true and a fictional past, and to treat its poets as legitimate historians. Whereas the Old Testament stories, embodying revealed truth, required belief, Homer made no claim to absolute truth at all.[6] And Hesiod admitted that the Muses "know how to speak many lies which are like the truth."[7] It was not until the Renaissance that historical criticism began to recognize the poetic character of the Mosaic narrative, that John Colet, for example, was able to think of God speaking to the early Hebrews about their origins in terms of a "holy fiction."[8] Even then, *historia sacra* retained for most interpreters a literal authority that inhibited inquiry into the poetic nature of the story it told.

Meanwhile, medieval exegetes had complicated the problem. By recognizing the value of the ancient fables, when allegorically interpreted, as moral philosophy teaching by example, they nourished the conviction that a history need not be true at all in any objective sense provided it be edifying and sufficiently verisimilar to be convincing. The perception that a fable, if true to life, could express an exemplary truth similar to that for which history was traditionally held responsible continued throughout the succeeding age to blur the distinction between history and imaginative expression, especially as it pertained to the past of myth and legend.

Renaissance commentators were thus left to deal with truth in historical poetry as an unresolved problem. Once beyond the absolute authority of sacred history, they had to find their way through a fog of uncertainty and ambivalence. To borrow Vives again as a witness for English humanism, the problem of truth in historical poetry seems to have concerned him deeply. References to it crop up with significant frequency throughout his voluminous critique of Western culture. Characteristically, he gave the problem itself a distinctly historical setting. Although he came, eventually, to appreciate the literary and moral value of the ancient poets, he could not excuse them entirely for adulterating the history of the earliest times with inventions he insisted on labeling "lies."[9] But he realized that their legacy had to be seen in relation to the age in which they lived. In a dialogue devoted to the problem of poetic license, he drew a sharp line at the first Olympiad. As a compromise between the positions taken by the personae "Truth" and "Falsehood"—proposed, significantly, by Homer, Hesiod, Lucian, and Apuleius, who, as successors of the earliest poets, Amphion, Orpheus, and the rest, he elsewhere castigated as dealers in lies—it was agreed that poets are permitted to mix invention with truth in their treatment of anything that took place before that time on the ground that what is known of that disturbed and obscure period is mostly fabulous anyway. For events after that date, however, Truth must prevail, except for certain embellishments in the interests of beauty, pleasure, or public utility.[10] Vives was here clearly groping for a formula that would legitimize historical poetry.

If the primary problem of Renaissance literary criticism was to justify imaginative literature,[11] the problem of more immediate concern involves the role of imaginative literature as an interpreter of prehistory. Both problems flourished in the atmosphere created during the sixteenth century by a revolution in the perception of "truth" itself. Conditioned in part by the tradition of Aristotelian empiricism, in part by the closely related utilitarian strain in English humanism, the new epistemology was expressed in, among other things, a compulsion to rationalize and historicize. With reference to the mythic past, this meant explaining the ancient myths in terms congruent with reason and experience, explaining away the obviously fabulous, and, regardless of the strain it might impose on the will to believe, giving it all a setting that, if not plausibly historical, was at least plausibly human. Whereas the allegorist was willing to eschew the literal meaning of a historical fable in the interests of whatever transcendent meaning he might wring from it, the historian (quite possibly the same person wearing his other hat) was just as ready to abandon the letter of the narrative in the interests of what he could accept as a rational explanation. Thus Europa's bull could readily become a ship identified with a bull, and the centaurs the first cavalry. The historicizer, moreover, had to have documentation whether he was dealing with supposed fact or romance: indeed the distinction between the two tended to dissolve in the curiously persistent quasi-empirical demand for bogus documentation in works of fiction.[12] Authors of romances were seemingly as concerned as historians to make it clear that they were not purveying "lies." The habit of insisting that fictional stories derived from some authentic source, usually an old manuscript, was no mere literary trick but a witness to the "truth" the story was supposed to convey. Though by no means a new manifestation—remember Geoffrey of Monmouth's *vetustissimus liber*—the custom of bogus documentation reflected a mind-set paradoxically conducive to both belief in a legendary past and respect for empirical scholarship. True, there were some who recognized it as bogus and, like More in *Utopia,* treated it with tongue in cheek or, like Rabelais, as a big joke. But historical thought had some maturing to do before "romance" could be automatically equated with "fancy." Meanwhile there existed a wide and ill-marked area between the truth of history and the truth of mere verisimilitude, of truth-to-the-life, that remained the uncontested, though not exclusive, province of the poet.

The most serious problem for Renaissance authors arose, however, not so much in distinguishing between simple truth and falsehood as in assaying the relative content of truth where ostensibly historical accounts moved beyond what could be determined according to the best standards of scholarship, especially those that crossed the line into prehistory or dealt with early times where documentation was scant or entirely lacking. Renaissance authors found their models among classical historians, who were refreshingly free to enhance their accounts with imagined speeches. As biographers, these authors were beginning to recognize that, to paint a convincing portrait, one had to fill in details not provided by specific documentation. From More to Bacon, practitioners in that evolving genre learned to tell a convincing story, and to interpret motive, by a more or less judicious use of the historical imagination.[13] It was becoming ever clearer that a coherent reconstruction of the past required the ability to establish a hitherto unknown point from known ones, a sort of intellectual triangulation, something like what modern historians take for granted as the process of interpretation.

The difficulty of reconciling history and imaginative literature, then generally categorized as poetry, naturally increased exponentially as inquiry into the prehistoric past was left largely, if not entirely, at the mercy of poets, be they the mythmakers of classical antiquity or the bards who transmitted the legends of Britain's own prehistory. The problem presented by poets as makers of myth and transmitters of legend was, of course, as old as antiquity itself. Ever since the Greeks began to examine the foundations of their own religion, they had recognized that poets had been its interpreters, if not its creators.[14] If the gods had indeed lived in historical time, the poets were at least responsible for their apotheosis. And medieval authors found the idea not only persuasive but in full accord with their own antipagan sentiments. As euhemerizers, the poets had become the agents of idolatry. But never had the poets' role as creators of the gods been more consistently taken for granted or set more clearly in historical context than in the Renaissance years.

The question concerning the role of poets in the euhemerizing process arose naturally enough as a result of the heightened interest being taken in the history of religion. In the course of his critique of contemporary culture, Vives went out of his way to stress the relation of poets to both ancient pagan religion and that of the Judaeo-Christian tradition, though whether, in the case of the former, he considered them as creators of the gods or merely celebrants is not clear.[15] No such ambiguity seems to have blunted the effect of later comments, however. George Puttenham, for example, assumed that the ancient poets, as euhemerizers, were in fact responsible for conferring divinity upon those mortals worthy of it. The muses, Spenser wrote, made Hercules and Bacchus immortal, and poets "glorified great men to heaven."[16] According to Thomas Heywood, it was "opinion" that made gods; and he undertook to show in dramatic form "how these (first born mortal) Gods were made / By virtue of divinest Poesie."[17] To Bacon, the gods were the product of the poets' effort to personify the elements of an arcane wisdom.[18] And Stillingfleet credited the Greek poets not only with working the euhemerized gods and heroes into a religion of idolatry, but with serving as agents in the process of a cultural transmission by which they were reputedly adapted from earlier mythologies.[19]

It was quite possible, however, to appreciate the role of poets as mythmakers, and to that extent to place the mythopoeic process in a relatively realistic historical perspective, without addressing the question of the "truth" embodied in legends of origin and quasi-historical myths. Not that many English authors were concerned with that question as a matter of high priority. But many were very much concerned with the more general problem of truth in poetic expression, and that problem inevitably involved the subcategory of historical truth. What precipitated the extended debate in Elizabethan England about truth in poetry was the puritanical attack on all imaginative literature. Strict observers, it is true, had always looked upon literature that deviated from the literal expression of fact as little better than lies and often referred to them as such, but certain among the variegated element in English society customarily lumped together as Puritan tended to take an extreme stand, condemning poetry as a category that included all imaginative literature.[20] The defensive attitude revealed by such apologists for poetic truth as Sir Philip Sidney suggests that there were still others who found it hard to think of fictitious narrative as anything but untruth. Legends and myths transmitted by poets as history naturally became especially vulnerable.

Renaissance authors of mythological manuals were themselves unlikely to give much guidance in distinguishing fiction from truth in the classical myths. Like their medieval predecessors, they preferred to introduce all quasi-historical fables with the finger-crossing phrase "Poets have feigned that . . ." Whether the phrase was meant to forewarn readers, or to denote something like the ordinary use of the imagination for which poets were traditionally licensed, or simply to disclaim responsibility for the literal veracity of a story that was in part at least obviously fabulous remains unclear. As a matter of fact, mythologers tended in time to make less use of the term "feigned," perhaps because it could be assumed to be understood; but the idea behind it hung like a cloud over the intentions of the authors, leaving ambiguous any question as to the historicity of the fables.

To speak more positively, the idea of "poesie historical" came in the late Elizabethan years to reflect the unspoken hope of bridging the gap between history as ascertained fact and the various imaginative evocations of a metahistorical past commonly identified with poetry. Although this idea, too, remained ambiguous—suspended somewhere between romance and that quality of imaginative interpretation which redeems history from "mere" fact—it nevertheless bore a deceptive weight of thought about the whole problem during that formative period before the more mature scholarship of the ensuing centuries had removed most of its inherent ambiguities. The immediate problem, then, is to dissect the hybrid concept of "poesie historical" as it appears in the writing of the English Renaissance.

Elizabethan interpreters were able to see the problem in a broader context than their predecessors. Not only had Aristotle's *Poetics* (available in print since early in the sixteenth century) provided them with a positive basis for the theoretical discussion of all poetry, in contrast to the largely negative assessment of it by the otherwise revered Plato, but they had also had practical experience in dealing with poetry as an expression of historical truth. In chapter 5, we have seen how investigation into the claims of Brutus and Arthur to historicity had provided unparalleled experience in the ways of "poets historical." Similarly, Spenser's efforts to explain Irish culture had taught him a good deal about "bards" as historical sources, and had suggested parallels between them and the ancient poets.[21] The historical-anthropological implications of the concept itself had broadened with the broadening of the geographical horizons. William Harrison found that bards who sang of "valiant princes, and fabulous narrations of the adulteries of the gods" not only were a common component of the societies the Romans called "barbarian," but had counterparts also in "new Spain."[22] Humanist biblical criticism no doubt also contributed to an understanding of the relationship between poetic expression and the making of myths. The poetic nature of Scripture had become well enough appreciated since the efforts of Petrarch and Boccaccio to legitimate poetic expression. Although the Reformation controversies left little leeway for anthropological speculation, Colet, for one, had been able to interpret Genesis in both historical and poetic terms. It was not so much that, by tempering the Divine Truth to the mentality of primitive tribesmen, Moses did for the Hebrews much the same service as the "poets" had done for the Gentiles (the "accommodation" theory had become common enough) as that he did it by "the bait of a holy fiction."[23] A century later, George Sandys was likewise able to see Moses in the same category as the "poets," except for the fact that *his* fiction was indeed holy.[24]

English critics were to find out, however, that defining the role of poets as interpreters of the mythic past was far from easy. Poets might be better able than historians to give extended meaning to historical events, but, in the process, truth as fact was only too likely to give way to a transcendent truth, and transcendence to allegory, thus escaping historical time altogether—unless, of course, the historian, like Bacon in his treatment of the wisdom inherent in the ancient myths, recognized the truth of allegory as in itself a historical manifestation worth pursuing as such. But this was a tendency more likely to affect the mythology of classical antiquity in which the putative historical content was shadowy to begin with. Poetic historicizing did better with regard to legends of more recent origin, and therefore close to what Bacon called "real history," where it simply enhanced an episode accepted as history rather than attaching some mythic meaning to it. In either case, the idea of "poesie historical" served, for lack of a better formula, as a bridge of sorts over the still murky area between history and myth.

What, then, did these English writers of the later sixteenth and early seventeenth centuries really mean by "poesie historical"? Though their answers may be neither clear nor convincing, they reveal much that is important about the dichotomous character, the ambivalence, of Renaissance thought and, more indirectly, about Renaissance perceptions of prehistory.

Already, perhaps as early as the late 1550s, George Puttenham had defined the idea with paradigmatic simplicity."[25] "Poesie historical" is, he wrote, "of all other [poetic forms] next the drama most honorable and worthy." It was a primary function of the poets' role as founders of civilization, as historians among the earliest peoples, and as praisers of famous men.[26] The poet historical, has, however, an advantage over the mere historian in that he need not adhere so closely to the facts known about the past. He may even "devise many historical matters of no veracity at all, but with purpose to do good," like "the commonwealth of Plato, and Sir Thomas More's Utopia." Thus historical poetry may be either wholly true, wholly false, or, as in Homer's "fabulous or mixed report" of the siege of Troy, a compound of both truth and falsehood.[27]

Later writers were to ring a variety of changes on this general theme. Of special importance was the wide area staked out for historical poetry between fact and fiction. Here again the influence of Aristotle's *Poetics* becomes apparent. If, according to Aristotle, poetry tends to express the universal and history the particular, and if the one relates what happened and the other what may happen or could have happened,[28] the poet could then more readily claim a truth of his own when dealing with experience, a certain verisimilitude related to fact but not limited by it, something transcendent and universal yet true to life, a truth that reflects probability if not certainty. It was a truth historians would one day partially subsume under the concept of interpretation, leaving the wholly unfettered use of the imagination to poets. For the time being, however, the "poet historical" could lay credible claim to the as yet ill-defined region between fact and fiction.

Sir Philip Sidney, as the most illustrious of the defenders of poetry, sought to claim that area for the poet without necessarily assigning him the qualifying title of "poet historical." This is not surprising, since he was concerned primarily with history's rivalry with poetry as a bearer of truth. But his poet could clearly become historical in the Aristotelian sense that he was able to give universal meaning to the particular facts with which the historian, "captived to the truth of the foolish world," is condemned to labor.[29] This higher truth, moreover, not only transcends historical fact but, as Puttenham had also argued, need not always conform to it where there is a valid—that is, a moral—reason for not doing so. The "feigned" Aeneas of Virgil, for example, is superior to the "right" Aeneas of Dares Phrygius because he is "more doctrinable."[30] Sidney spoke of the heroes as revealed in the Greek dramas in the same breath with Chaucer's pilgrims and More's *Utopia*[31]—he could just as well have included the heroic inventions of his own *Arcadia.* All, in any case, shared a certain truth-to-life that, according to the elastic license he and others among his fellow Elizabethans accorded the poet historical, could qualify as history. On the other hand, and more realistically, he pointed out that even the ordinary historian must depart from fact in order to tell a coherent story: "Many times he must tell events whereof he can yield no cause, or if he do, it must be poetically."[32]

Whether the broad franchise Sidney gave to poets as interpreters of that element of historical truth that transcended historical fact supported actual belief in the myths they wrote about is, of course, another matter. To find something "doctrinable" in the careers of the gods and heroes of the Homeric and Hesiodic tradition,[33] or to endorse the hyperbolic notion that Homer and Hesiod had passed on to later ages "all knowledge, logic, rhetoric, philosophy natural and moral" under the veil of fable,[34] was not necessarily to accept those fables as historically true, even in part. Indeed, Sidney at one point lumped "heroes and demigods" together with "cyclops, chimeras, furies and the like" that "never were in nature," as alike beyond the range of the historian, and presumably also beyond credence as history.[35]

More than either Puttenham or Sidney, Spenser explored the parameters of "poesie historical." Whereas Puttenham simply gave fresh statement to some venerable ideas, and Sidney viewed the subject ironically in the distorting light of debate, Spenser was himself the very model of a "poet historical." As poet and part-time historian, he had experience with both aspects of the hybrid concept, and he revealed in practice the contradictions inherent in it. In addition, he seems to have recognized more clearly than most of his contemporaries the importance of defining it. To him, the "poet historical" was one who mediated between history and the legendary past. In the great tradition of epic poetry, he sought in *The Faerie Queene* to make sense out of experience by revealing the order that he perceived in it,[36] yet he hoped to keep the process from degenerating into abstraction by associating it with the legendary history of Britain. He planned to transmute the national legends, considered for the purposes of poetic expression as history, into the more rarified substance of myth—of myth, that is, not as embodied in the ancient fables, but, more nearly in the modern sense, as an ordering of the national community's memory to provide inspiration for both present and future—in this instance for the dual purpose of glorifying the reign of Elizabeth and "fashioning a gentleman or noble person in virtuous and gentle discipline." In his well-known letter to Ralegh, he tells quite frankly what he was up to. Following "all the antique Poets historical," from Homer and Virgil to Ariosto and Tasso, he planned his own epic as a "historical fiction" such as would serve as the structure of his "continued allegory and dark conceit."[37] He would feature the historical Arthur insofar as he was reflected in the familiar "Briton moniments" (i.e., the British History), but, as poet, he would feel free to use his imagination and also to draw upon the bogus documentation embodied in the "Antiquities of Faerie land," which "no body can know."[38] Spenser's "poet historical" was thus deeply engaged in the nation's past, but it was the past of legend, not of objective history; and his franchise remained more than a little ambiguous, involving as it did a set of legends, which he apparently did not really believe, and a dynastic myth that was validated by history but not bound by it. His task was to explore the transcendent meaning of history, not the facts. For Spenser, poetry was the language of myth, and he treated his "Briton moniments" with a license so truly poetical as to link them rather to the "antiquities of Faerie land" than to the British History.

When, however, he came to write as "historiographer," in the course of his effort to unravel the early history of Ireland, he virtually denied the historical truth supposedly contained in all bardic legends of origin, "it being as impossible to prove that there was ever such Brutus of England, as it is, that there was any such Gathelus of Spain."[39] Yet he let the legend of Brutus stand in the genealogies he incorporated in his epic poem.[40] Although he found the analogous legends transmitted by Irish bards "mere fables and very Milesian lies," he could not help agreeing with many of his contemporaries that, even so, "under these tales ye may in a manner see the truth lurk."[41]

Clearly, then, Spenser came no nearer than Sidney to an accommodation between poetic history and history proper. True, he was himself able to serve both as "poet historical" and "historiographer," but he apparently acted on the assumption that the two differed fundamentally, both in method and purpose. He treated the same material very differently according to whether his own purpose was primarily poetical or historical, whether, that is, he was writing poetical history or history from poetical sources.[42] Nor was he sure how the element of truth embodied in bardic legend, British or Irish, related to the truth to which he undertook to give mythic interpretation in his epic poem.

If Spenser was poet first and historian a distant second, the reverse was true of his friend Ralegh. It was Ralegh who revealed from the historian's point of view the nature and limitations inherent in the idea of "poesie historical"—by implication, that is, for he was concerned primarily with the problem of what to do with the ancient poets as historical sources. In this, as in so many other respects, he reflected the Elizabethan mind and temper. Although he accepted the evidence of the Greek poets with some reluctance, preferring what he believed to be the incontrovertible evidence of the Bible, he had nothing against poets as such: he agreed with Sidney that historians themselves must at times think like poets and that they in fact "do borrow of poets, not only much of their ornament, but somewhat of their substance."[43] He knew, in other words, that to piece together the fragments left from past ages must be, in part, a work of the imagination. Unlike Sidney, however, he made no invidious distinction between the roles of poet, philosopher, and historian, assuming, indeed, that they were mutually supportive.[44] He simply considered "the poets" less authoritative than the Mosaic story. At best they represented a corruption of that record, and their gods and heroes were merely distant echoes of the personages told of therein.[45] Both traditions he sought to make believable in human terms; but whereas he tried, by elaborately imaginative rationalization, to fill in the cryptic outline of Genesis—the story of the Flood, for example—he felt quite free to criticize the ancient poets.

In fact, Ralegh treated the poets with a mixture of scorn, skepticism, and a grudging realization that their fables had somehow to be reconciled with the main line of universal chronology. They could not be ignored. Since he believed that the pagan authors had adapted their stories with irresponsible freedom from original Hebrew versions, they bore for him a certain reflected respectability.[46] And, as Spenser found out in the case of the Irish legends, the poetic sources helped fill in otherwise troublesome lacunae in the authoritative record. This process, Ralegh realized, did not always contribute to the truth. Just as mapmakers fill in spaces they know nothing about with strange creatures and "mathematical lines," so, he wrote, did the Greek historians and poets "embroider and intermix the tales of ancient times with a world of fictions and fabulous discoveries."[47] On the other hand, like the skillful chemist who can separate good things from poison, so may "those which seek after God and Truth find out everywhere, and in all the ancient Poets and Philosophers, the story of the first Age . . . amply and lively expounded."[48] Much the same was true with regard to the later legends—those, for example, having to do with the Trojan War: despite "strange fables" and "allegories far strained," "such [persons] as can either interpret their fables, or separate them from the naked truth, shall find matter in Poems, not unworthy to be regarded of historians."[49]

A similar ambivalence affected the more erudite and prosaic Selden, who in his earlier career had reason to confront the problem of poetical history. The task of annotating Drayton's *Poly-Olbion*—which, by the way, he accepted with some misgivings[50]—brought him face to face with the unreconstructed British History and required him to give thought specifically to poetical history as an interpreter of legend. Like most of his contemporaries, he was of two minds about it—unequal, but dual nonetheless.[51] He had as good reason as Spenser, perhaps better, to be skeptical of legends that originated with unlettered bards and were transmitted by them, but, as Spenser himself found out, the resulting story could not be totally ignored. He claimed not to be against poetic sources as such, and for his own work he made a point of using all available materials "as well verse as prose."[52] He was, indeed, a pioneer in a kind of cultural history that had been sadly neglected by the Tudor chroniclers and that recognized no arbitrary limitations. Yet he gave only grudging license to the poet as historian. He had serious doubts about Drayton's retelling of a story already hopelessly garbled by "bardish imposture." Of Brutus and the Trojan myth, he wrote with ironic tolerance: since no nation "can justify itself but by tradition, . . . you shall enough please Saturn and Mercury, presidents of antiquity and learning, if with the author you foster this belief."[53] And he set it as his own duty "to explain the author, carrying himself . . . as an historical poet," and to "insert oft, out of the British story, what I importune you not to credit."[54] He had deep doubts, for example, about such things as prophecies and portents. Yet he granted, somewhat vaguely, that a poet "may well guess the like."[55] Selden, in short, tended to solve the knotty problem of poetic history simply by cutting it in two.

It was left to Bacon to develop the idea of poetical history within a more philosophical context and with special reference to the ancient myths.[56] He had, in fact, articulated his theory of myth initially with reference to poetry as a branch of learning. Having limited himself to poetry considered exclusively as "feigned history"—which ruled out "Satires, Elegies, Epigrams, Odes, and the like"—he proposed to treat the subject under three categories: "Narrative, Dramatic, and Parabolic." Whereas narrative poetry "is a mere imitation of history," and dramatic "is as history made visible," parabolic poetry "is typical history, by which ideas that are objects of the intellect are represented in poems that are objects of the sense."[57]

As Bacon describes it, narrative poetry is the breeder of legend. "Since the acts and events which are the subjects of real history are not," he insisted, "of sufficient grandeur to satisfy the human mind, Poetry is at hand to feign acts more heroical; since the successes and issues of actions as related in true history are far from being agreeable to the merits of virtue and vice, Poesy corrects it."[58] Combined with music, this kind of poetry was held in honor "even in the rudest ages and among barbarous people, when other kinds of learning were utterly exhausted."[59] Parabolic poetry, on the other hand, composed in terms of parables and fables, constituted for Bacon the natural medium for mythic expression, and helped him explain the part played by myth in a prerational, prehistoric age. Though it had nothing more than incidentally to do with "real" or "true" history, parabolic poetry expressed what early ages considered most sacred, much as parables came to be used for religious teaching in the Christian tradition. And, though it lent itself to corruption "by the levity and idleness of wits in dealing with allegory,"[60] it was the medium peculiarly appropriate to allegorical expression, and hence for the wisdom Bacon was convinced lay hidden within the pagan myths.

Bacon, moreover, refused to be confused about the exemplary function poetic history shared with history proper. In their search for the truth that history was supposed to teach by example, Renaissance authors found it hard, as had their medieval forebears, to distinguish the exemplary truth of myth and romance from the exemplary function of history. As noticed above, Puttenham had maintained that the poet historical could perform his historical function by devising "many historical matters of no verity at all, but with purpose to do good." Sidney agreed, and propounded the further paradox that a false version of a historical episode could be truer than a factual one if made more "doctrinable" by poetic—that is, imaginative—treatment.[61] Bacon no doubt agreed also, up to a point, but he was more discriminating in his handling of examples. At one point he declared that those derived from poetical history are only "substitutes and supplements of examples," good enough for a time before "true history" had provided "living examples."[62] He still, however, justified legend as a poetic extension of history for the pragmatic purposes of public policy, deliberately meant to enhance the prestige of a regime.[63]

Aside from the problem of "truth" in poetical history, the concept of "poesie historical" itself presented a problem. As suggested at an earlier point in this chapter, it appears to have reflected an unspoken hope that a bridge might be constructed between history as ascertained fact and the various imaginative evocations of a metahistorical past more commonly associated with poetry. The odds, however, were against any such hope. Though the idea of writing poetical history—of actually combining history and poetry, not merely making use of occasional historical themes as the subject for poetical or dramatic treatment—had teased the Elizabethan taste, and continued to do so in the less inspiring climate of Jacobean England, efforts to write it were not proving very satisfactory. Daniel, who probably tried hardest to make such a synthesis work, gave it up and turned to writing history in prose. Drayton, who undertook the ambitious project of poeticizing Camden's *Britannia* together with the legendary history of England, tacitly admitted the impossibility of combining history and poetry by asking Selden, as a young scholar of rising reputation, to annotate his *Poly-Olbion* from the historian's point of view so that he might leave himself free to serve more freely in his chosen capacity as poet. The concept of "poesie historical," in fact, remained stubbornly dichotomous: a Renaissance-type compromise, a hybrid condemned to sterility by the perceived incompatibility of its parents. For poetical history to have served such an interpretive purpose would have required accepting both the right and the ability of the historical imagination to confer upon the myth-history of the ancient poets and the legends transmitted by native bards whatever legitimacy might be consistent with reason and experience. In other words, it would require Renaissance minds to realize, as modern historians have come to realize, that all historiography involves the participation of the imagination—even, as historians have been told more recently, an element of poetry. But that, in turn, would have necessitated a clearer understanding of the historical imagination itself and of the relation of poetry to history than most thinkers of the time were able to achieve. The relation of imagination to poetry was then clear enough; not so its relation to history.

For beneath the dichotomy represented by "poesie historical," troublesome enough in itself, lay a more profound dichotomy. According to the traditional and still prevailing "faculty" psychology, poetry was considered a function of "imagination" and history of "memory." If taken at face value, this distinction would have ensured the complete irreconcilability of poetry and history. Fortunately for both, it was accorded more lip service than consistent application. Bacon, for example, took the faculty psychology for granted as the framework for his grand scheme for the reorganization of learning, but he eventually came to see how inapplicable it was to man's actual thought processes. But Bacon's is an exceptional example. Insofar as the traditional psychology remained paradigmatic, the imagination continued to be associated with poetry. Yet it was becoming more and more apparent that, if historians were to reach beyond the "mouse-eaten records" with which Sidney preferred to picture them as "loaded,"[64] it would have to be by means of the imagination—especially as it allowed them to arrive at that likelihood of truth which was essential to any coherent picture of the earliest ages.

The importance of probability was not lost upon contemporary thinkers. In the course of his efforts to make sense out of the stories left inadequately told in Scripture and mythology, Ralegh came to realize that a probability of truth, even when arrived at imaginatively—"poetically" he preferred to call it—was better than no credible story at all; nor, he argued, should such a story, though admittedly the product of "conjecture," be considered "feigning," like the more fabulous of the ancient fables.[65] Spenser came to much the same conclusion as he attempted to wring some "likelihood of truth . . . a probability of things" about Irish origins from legends handed down from an unlettered age by highly imaginative bards.[66] The principle of probability, it would seem, could go a long way toward relieving the imagination from any exclusive relationship to poetry, and toward legitimizing "poesie historical" as an interpretive concept.

Spenser's experience with legendary history also led him closer to an understanding of how historical interpretation could arise from the kind of sources most dependent upon the imaginative quest for probability. He came to see that the "likelihood of truth" he hoped to find would require supplementing and checking the bardic traditions "by comparison of times, likeness of manners and customs, affinity of words and names, properties of natures and uses, resemblances of sites and ceremonies, monuments of churches and tombs."[67] Bacon, too, was able to envision the historian imaginatively reconstructing the more distant past from "antiquities." Although he considered such materials secondary to those involved in what he called "civil history," they would, he argued, make it possible for historians "to carry the mind . . . back into the past, and to bring it into sympathy with antiquity."[68] They were the impersonal remains that, "like spars of a shipwreck," could be made to "recover somewhat from the deluge of time."[69]

But the nearer both he and Spenser, each in his own way, came to a methodological scheme that might embrace "poesie historical" and perhaps resolve its dichotomy, the clearer it becomes that the riddle itself has escaped unresolved. It begins, indeed, to appear that neither one had any such resolution in mind in the first place. Spenser apparently meant his method for dealing with poeticized legends not so much to support them as to exorcise the poetic element in them or, but for the residue of fact he still believed they contained, to circumvent them. And Bacon is explicit in his hope that historical learning, as he envisioned it, would "supersede the fabulous [i.e., poetic] accounts of the origins of nations."[70]

Useful enough in theory, "poesie historical" tended, in actual discussion, to fall apart, the relation of the poetic component to the historical depending on the viewpoint of the participant. In the heat of argument, Sidney could go so far as to assert that "the best of the historian is subject to the Poet" because the latter, "having all Dante's heaven and hell under authority of his pen,"[71] can place the historian's supposedly sterile record in perspective *sub specie aeternitatis*. Bacon, on the other hand, never doubted that all interpretations, including poeticized history, should be the historian's responsibility. Spenser tried to have it both ways, but in the process revealed how intractably dichotomous the notion of "history poetical" really was. Whether in his own writings he was acting as "poet historical" or "historiographer" depended on his immediate purpose: whereas, in *The Faerie Queene,* he was himself engaged in writing poetical history, in his Irish studies he was trying to distill history from poetical sources. At times he could treat the very same materials quite differently according to which hat he was wearing.[72]

In this respect, as in so many others, Bacon occupies a special place and presents a special problem. In his scheme of things, the dichotomy inherent in "poesie historical" and the potentially invidious distinction between imagination and memory were no longer matters of primary concern. Indeed, there is reason to believe that he was becoming well aware of the artificiality of the traditional faculty psychology. Once, in a moment of apparently relaxed insight, he admitted that all intellectual activity was alike in that it involved thought, which was something that was bound to transcend arbitrary categories: "For he who remembers or recollects thinks; he who imagines thinks; he who reasons thinks."[73]

Moreover, he was clearly less interested in the truth of poetical history than in its historical-anthropological implications. He accorded the ancient poets a legitimate, if strictly secondary, place in his scheme for historical learning, but associated them with a prerational age, an age of myth.[74] By the same token, he was more interested in the myths themselves as expressions of a universal and timeless wisdom than as possible historical sources. While agreeing with his contemporaries that a kernel of truth might lie within them, he also shared enough of the skepticism increasingly apparent in the intellectual climate[75] to cause him to play down their historical value. Whatever hard history they might contain he held incidental to their allegorical message, at best a happy windfall for the historian.[76]

If Bacon's fascination with "the wisdom of the ancients" may seem more nearly a regression to medieval allegorism than a forecast of the modern fascination with archetypes, his willingness to study the ancient myths also as windows into the mind of the age that produced them[77] points rather to the future, a future in which historical-anthropological thought was to move so far beyond the notion of "poesie historical" as to render it obsolete.

"Poesie historical" may have failed as a heuristic device, but it represents a crucial phase in the evolution of historical thought. It served, for a while, as the focal point for most discussion of the mythic and legendary past. As it matured in the course of such discussion, it involved something more than the rival claims of poetry and history, of imagination and memory. As it came inevitably to bear upon prehistory, on the ancient "poets" and the bardic sources of national legend, it reflected a crisis of belief in the face of a past that was largely unknowable, yet which had in some measure to be made known. As a result—perhaps the most important result—those who spoke the language of "poesie historical" found themselves ultimately forced to recognize for what it was that gray area of historical truth that involved probability, verisimilitude, truth-to-life, and reasoned conjecture, and in the process to adumbrate principles of historical thought that did not take fully modern shape until a later period. As such, the concept of "poesie historical" tided historical consciousness over a difficult stage in the perception of a prehistory shadowed in ancient myth, and of the nation's own prehistory then barely emerging from the mists of legend. It came close to providing a working formula for contestants in the debate over the British History who had to winnow whatever grain of probable truth they could from bardic verse. In theory, however, the idea remained stubbornly dichotomous, ready to separate into its component elements in response to the flow of debate. Bacon, alone of his compatriots, recognized that a satisfactory historical approach to the past, especially the primitive past, would require that the historical component be made to subsume whatever there might be either of probability or transcendent truth in the poetic.

A product of literary discussion, "poesie historical" failed long to outlive its origin. The fact is that circumstances in post-Baconian England were not favorable to "poesie historical," either as a genre or an interpretive concept. Poeticized history had flourished in the Elizabethan sunlight, but poetry itself was now having to adapt to a climate less conducive to its uses in historical thought. The historical drama that for Elizabethans had given poetic interpretation to the national history was in decline and was soon to disappear, with the stage itself, during the years of Puritan domination. The Elizabethan taste for versified history, exemplified by the ambitious projects of Daniel and Drayton, was succumbing to disillusionment. Daniel left his history of the Civil Wars unfinished and turned instead to the writing of prose history, and Drayton was disappointed with the reception of his *Poly-Olbion.* A new kind of poetry was taking shape, a poetry more nearly in tune with real history and the temper of the Royal Society than with the mythical and legendary past.

Historians, for their part, and those, more numerous, who were users of history were gaining a clearer sense of what they were doing and what determined the scope of history. Events during the turbulent Renaissance years had posed questions that could be answered only by reaching beyond the mere record of events into the past of ideas, beliefs, and customs, even into the most distant past then known only through "the poets." Historians were thus gradually assuming a de facto responsibility for that element of probability, of versimilitude, of truth-to-life, which constituted whatever claim "poesie historical" might have had to historical truth. Still more to the point, the putative ability of "poesie historical" to mediate between the truth of reason and the truth of fable, which would have been essential to its status as a heuristic device, was becoming more and more difficult to achieve in the light of the newly rigorous rationalism of the later seventeenth and eighteenth centuries.

Conclusion and a Glance Ahead

The foregoing studies have been devoted primarily to three related problems: first, the shifting balance of belief and skepticism regarding the historical content traditionally thought to inhere in ancient myth and national legend, a problem involving, in particular, the decline and fall of euhemerism; second, a dawning awareness of myth and mythmaking as in themselves aspects of the history of civilization, regardless of their putative historical content; and third, the emergence of a source of myth unrelated to either the classical myth-history or the mythology emanating from *historia sacra* and in some respects more useful than either as a source of historical perspective then thought so important in the discussion of secular affairs.

While shifting perceptibly in the direction of skepticism, the balance between belief in the historicity of the mythic and legendary history and doubt, verging on outright disbelief, remained uncertain. Euhemerism emerges from the Renaissance years fatally weakened but far from dead: the gods have been effectively challenged as historical figures, but even in the most skeptical minds there still stirs the nagging thought that some element of truth lurks beneath the veil of fable, or the feeling that if only more were known, especially about the legendary history of England, more of it would be found to be in accord with reason and the evidence of experience. And there remains, in certain quarters, a will to believe so powerful as to override rational criticism yet stubbornly devoted to rationalizing the irrational and making credible the incredible.

That ambivalence should have characterized much of this kind of thinking, and on as evanescent and equivocally documented a subject as the prehistory shrouded in myth and legend, should come as no surprise. Renaissance minds seem to have been especially susceptible to ambivalence. Faced with newly complex issues arising in a society undergoing more than ordinarily rapid change, a society that was itself a tissue of contradictions, thinking persons, when not directed by imposed dogma, could be only too ready to find truth in opposites and to take a perverse satisfaction in paradox. More surprising is the fact that, in such circumstances, they could come as often as they did to attitudes that would one day mature into new ideas.

Fundamentally, however, ambivalence arose out of confusion about the nature of historical truth itself. Renaissance minds inherited diverse, even contradictory, modes of belief. They still tended to draw an indistinct line between documentable fact and "truth-to-life." Moreover, that which enjoyed the authority of tradition, of consensus over the ages, could not easily be ignored despite evidence to the contrary: hence the tendency, especially apparent in discussion of Britain's legendary origins, for reputable scholars to present both the legend and its critics and to let those believe who would. Belief, indeed, depended to an appreciable extent on the character of discussion: it seems to have been possible, in the context of conventional rhetoric, to treat a myth in apparent seriousness as if it were history, yet, in the context of experience and reason, to deny its historicity. To acknowledge that "the poets" had "feigned" a story apparently did little to deter euhemerists from assuming that a kernel of truth remained within the shell of fable.

Such variant expressions of belief depended on the further belief that the ancient myths could be made believable as history by explaining away the supernatural element in them and reducing them to terms more in accord with things as they were currently observed. Efforts to rationalize and historicize no doubt kept the myths alive in historical thought: they made it possible for the neo-euhemerists of the late seventeenth and early eighteenth centuries still to take the pagan gods seriously as historical figures. But the improbabilities that inevitably remained just as surely contributed to the skepticism increasingly apparent in Elizabethan and Jacobean thought. Willing, even eager, as readers of that period undoubtedly were, to suspend disbelief—the gods of Olympus were, after all, an important part of their cultural heritage, and England's legendary heroes still occupied a respected place in historiography—it was becoming even clearer to intellectuals that both myth and legend had been filtered through successive layers of poetic imagination. In either case, efforts to make the fabulous believable could only raise doubts concerning their historicity. Given the inertia of tradition, however, demystifying the mythical past, like the analogous process of rationalizing sacred history, was bound to be slow.

With reference to the second problem—the recognition of myth and mythmaking as aspects, in their own right, of the history of mankind—the story is, if not crystal clear, at least less plagued by ambivalence. As they learned more about the nature and history of man, some perceptive observers seem to have shifted whatever attention they saw fit to pay to prehistory from the exploits of the gods to the myths themselves and to the mythopoeic process as evidence of a stage in the history of civilization—an age of myth through which, they were coming to believe, all peoples had at one time to pass through, an age characterized by a primitive mentality, one, moreover, that tended to express itself in poetical and parabolic terms rather than in rational discourse. The idea of an age of myth and poetry stemmed from classical antiquity, from Varro in particular, but it received fresh support from contemporary perceptions of social evolution. The American aborigines, and, as England's own antiquity clarified, the ancient Britons as well, seemed to provide concrete evidence for what would otherwise have remained a troublesomely abstract conception of the primitive. Controversy over the historicity of the national legends and discussion about the nature of poetry itself drew attention as never before to the part played by oral tradition in the transmission of myth and legend. Discerning minds were coming to recognize that the ancient myths had been handed down orally long before they were written down and that the national legends had been initially the work of "unlettered bards"—though defenders of the medieval tradition remained reluctant to abandon the notion that the ancient peoples of Britain had had letters "ab initio." Interest in hieroglyphics, moreover, was lending perspective to the evolution of language and, more particularly, to the symbolic thinking believed to characterize the primitive mind. Simplistic as much of this kind of speculation was bound to be, it nevertheless opened up intriguing vistas to the historical imagination and, by focusing on collective mentalities and societies rather than on personages, it tended to free contemplation of the earliest times from the tyranny of genealogical chronology.

The bleaker primitivism of the "cave myth" was similarly dependent on both ancient authority and the vision of contemporary savagery and similarly free from the limitations inherent in a genealogical time scheme. But, if anything, it bore broader implications than the idea of an age of myth. Though entirely speculative—and therefore infinitely adaptable—the idea that mankind in "the first age" lived a totally exiguous, quasi-feral existence in caves and forests and was brought only by gradual steps to a state of comparative civility in fact served a variety of authors, especially those who concerned themselves with contemporary problems, as the historical perspective they needed for public discussion of all sorts. The cave myth no doubt commended itself in large part because it allowed its users to bypass the more conventional formulas. Largely independent of both biblical history and the history myths of classical antiquity, it was essentially secular, a fact that added significantly to its adaptability both then and later. Since primitive man, thus envisioned, had nowhere to go but up, the cave myth became obviously developmental in its implications, though if it had not been for the concurrent appreciation of the similarly developmental implications of the changes increasingly noticed in contemporary society, those of the cave myth might have seemed less obvious. As it was, that myth was able to circumvent the two most antidevelopmental myths then still popular, those of the Golden Age and the decay of nature.

What drew English scholars and men of letters to the prehistory embodied in myth and legend was less an interest in the subject itself than concern for something else to which it was more or less indirectly related. The literary scholars of the later Elizabethan years who discussed the nature and scope of poetry, including its relation to history, did more than would seem to have been their share to clarify the problem of historical truth in myth. Their hopefully debated principle of "poesie historical," it is true, failed in the long run to mediate satisfactorily between the historian's claim to fact and the poet's claim to a truth that transcended it, but in the process they became aware of the extent to which those rival jurisdictions overlapped, and of the broad if ill-marked area in which probability, conjecture, and verisimilitude promised a valid means of interpreting raw fact. If, as Bacon recognized, such interpretation led more toward history than poetry, and if, as a result, the concept tended to separate into its component parts, that tendency assured historians the maximum access to whatever portion of myth and legend remained open to rational criticism. Again, the battle of books that raged during most of the sixteenth century over the historicity of the British History performed a similar service. Stung by criticism of the legends about the origins of Britain and about its eponymous heroes launched from the superior vantage point of humanist scholarship, patriotic English and Welsh antiquaries mounted a defense so radical in its acceptance of the traditional version as to force all concerned to face more squarely than had ever been possible the problem of truth in legend.

As in so many other aspects of Renaissance thought, understanding in this respect lasted longer with regard to the historicity of the classical myths than in the case of the British History controversy or the debate over the problem of "poesie historical," largely because the ancient myths did not become involved in such an open, and up to a point decisive, controversy as did those latter issues that touched a sensitive nerve in the contemporary mind. Not that the ancient mythology was ignored. On the contrary, it continued to provide the symbolic language for all public discussion. The standard manuals continued to mix euhemerism and allegory in a thoroughly conservative blend. And, with the help of foreign scholars, a few English scholars were busily at work synthesizing pagan mythology and biblical history; but whatever debate they stirred up bore on the respective time schemes as they stood rather than on the historicity of either.

It would seem that these latter scholars, and especially their successors of the late seventeenth and early eighteenth centuries with their relatively sophisticated philological learning and their obsession with universal chronology, might have continued the critical treatment of the ancient myth-history begun more informally by a few select minds of the Renaissance period. But when one moves into the later period in the hope of finding a logically satisfying conclusion to the unfinished battle between belief and skepticism and the ultimate defeat of euhemerism, one seems to be reaching for a step that is not there. If there is any truth at all to the adage that knowledge comes but wisdom lingers, it is surely borne out by the way scholars of post-Renaissance England dealt with the gods, demigods, and heroes of classical mythology. Heirs to an already rich philological and chronological learning and possessed of a hitherto unparalleled erudition, such scholars as Sir Isaac Newton, Bishop Cumberland, and, with qualifications, Samuel Shuckford and Bishop Warburton continued to take euhemerism happily for granted as an indication that the gods once actually walked the earth. In the course of an obsessive avocational interest in concocting a unified chronology, Newton, the scientist, gave free rein to a surprisingly unscientifc credulity and took his Ceres, his Bacchus his various Jupiters, and the rest quite at their face value. These *érudits,* to be sure, took the more preposterous aspects of the fables with magisterial discretion, using the time-worn rationalizations that were supposed to leave standing a believable history. Like many of his early eighteenth-century contemporaries, Shuckford recognized that euhemerism did not by itself explain the advent of the gods, but he, too, took their historicity on faith in his effort, typical of the English neo-euhemerists, to "connect" sacred and profane history.

English neo-euhemerists, it is true, did not differ in this respect greatly from their continental counterparts. The abbé Banier, the most popular of early eighteenth-century mythologists, though certainly more subtle than Newton and more eclectic, was no less positive in his acceptance of the euhemerized gods as historical figures. And, even if we grant that most of Newton's successors broadened their conception of euhemerism, the fact remains that euhemeristic historicizing continued to mark the work of most mythologists and chronographers throughout the first half of the century. Meanwhile, however, those more radical thinkers who were the early exponents of the Enlightenment, Bayle, Fontenelle, and, of course, Vico, were reinterpreting ancient religion on psychological grounds—the fears of primitive minds in the face of a universe not understood—rather than on the ancient habit of deifying dead men, and were in the process effectively destroying the historical credentials of the gods.

That the historicity of the gods should otherwise have retained such wide acceptance in an age commonly thought of as one peculiarly marked by devotion to reason may seem paradoxical, and in a sense it is. Yet the paradox is in some respects more apparent than real. Euhemerism itself was in essence a rationalizing concept, a device that made belief respectable for a society wary of the fabulous. As such, it had much in common with latitudinarian biblical exegesis, which likewise sought to support belief by making the

Scriptures accord as far as possible with experience. When viewed in a similarly rationalizing and historicizing perspective, gods and heroes, patriarchs and prophets had alike to be included in any plan meant to rationalize universal history. In either case, rationalization proceeded on premises ultimately acceptable only on faith—which may be paradox enough.

The remarkable thing about the neo-euhemerists of seventeenth- and early eighteenth-century England is not so much that they were, in this respect, representative of their age as that they seem to have been impervious to other aspects of it that might have altered their perspective. They ignored, in particular, the new ethnology which had already done much to shape English perceptions of prehistory and would one day revolutionize the study of primitive religion. Knowledge of the savage peoples of the New World, already widespread in England, could have provided them, as it did the more advanced of their French contemporaries, with thought-provoking parallels between savage customs and those thought to have characterized the earliest times. It might also have underscored for them the fact that euhemerism, far from legitimizing the ancient gods, was simply, but significantly, a phase in the evolution of primitive religion. That the neo-euhemerists apparently saw no reason to pay special attention to the new study of man surely tells something about the paradoxical juxtaposition of learning and credulity in their thinking.

It could be argued, indeed, that, in the story of the decline and fall of euhemerism, those select minds of Renaissance England who turned a critical eye on the ancient myth-history had more in common with the *philosophes* of the eighteenth century, who radically redirected the study of primitive man on the basis of the new anthropology, than with their more immediate successors with all their philological learning and chronological ingenuity.

Be that as it may, certain things about English Renaissance approaches to the mythic prehistory would no doubt have appealed to the *philosophes*. English intellectuals had already absorbed much of the anthropological knowledge that was to alter preconceptions about the primitive world. Elizabethan and Jacobean authors seldom missed an opportunity to use parallels drawn from what they had heard about American Indians—a tendency, by the way, especially apparent when they were invoking the cave myth. Although they took that vision of the solitary and exiguous life of primeval man in caves and forests initially from the ancients, they were quick to seize upon the American experience as collateral evidence. The *philosophes,* for their part, took their view of primitive man more from the Indians than from the ancients, despite a strong Lucretian strain in their thinking. But both they and the Renaissance thinkers ended up with a remarkably similar vision. When David Hume refers to primitive man as "a barbarous necessitous animal," he seems to be echoing Hobbes' famous comment on man's grim life in the state of nature, just as Hobbes was more certainly echoing a tradition already well mined.

Two things about the cave myth could have recommended it to the exponents of the Enlightenment: its secularity and its developmental implications. Renaissance commentators were not, of course, secular in the same anticlerical, free-thinking style frequently found among the *philosophes.* They had simply acquired, for more or less practical discourse, the habit of separating things human from things divine without in any serious way challenging accepted religious beliefs. But both found a measure of intellectual freedom in a view of primitive man and his social evolution that was unrestricted by the highly personalized and theologically exacting account of the Pentateuch. On the social evolution of man, exponents of the cave myth were likewise headed in the direction of Enlightenment thought. Condorcet would have found the confident assumption of evolution implied in the perception of man's rise from the primordial caves and forests an engagingly naive interpretation of a profound truth. If it did not amount to the explicit idea of progress he had in mind, it represented the kind of thinking he would have considered conducive to it.

The *philosophes* would also have found familiar the idea of a primitive collective mentality adumbrated by Renaissance authors as they sought to relate the evidence of American savagery to their perception of life in the first age, as well as to the only marginally less savage existence they were coming to believe characteristic of their own British ancestors. In the wake of the studies made by Fontenelle and Lafitau, certain eighteenth-century thinkers were coming to envision with unprecedented clarity a mentality common to all primitive peoples, whether ancient Greeks or contemporary savages. It was a mentality that expressed itself, somewhat as do children, in concrete images and stories rather than in rational discourse. This conception of man's earliest state in terms of mind and its corollary, the psychological explanation of primitive religion, shattered the monopoly of euhemerism without denying the historical significance of the myths as such. At the hands of Vico, the most perceptive prehistorian of the age, the myths became, indeed, not the personalized history of peoples in the earliest age, but symbols that represented their universal language and recorded their social development.

Changing the changeables of knowledge and sophistication of scholarship—this was the general direction in which a few English minds of the Renaissance were already traveling. Though they may have tended to think of primitive societies more in terms of the conditions of life than of mind, they could not long imagine a primitive life-style apart from a primitive mentality; nor, as Bacon found out, could the rise of myths be convincingly explained without reference to a mentality for which poetry and fable had to do the service of rational discourse.

In pursuit of a primitive mentality, Bacon and a few of his compatriots found themselves contemplating a chronology unlike the personalized and biblically oriented chronology to which the neo-euhemerists were devoted, but rather a sequence of ages that could serve as the framework for a history of civilization. Though they resorted, as Vico did a century later, to the time-honored division of history into the ages, successively, of gods, heroes, and men, the first age became for them one of myth—an age peculiarly given to expression in parabolic and hieroglyphic form, an age worth examining in and for itself without necessary regard to the specific content of the fables. If their approach to the ancient mythology did not immediately outlaw euhemerism it shifted the spotlight from the gods to the culture that gave rise to them in a way that, perhaps more than anything else, foreshadowed the Enlightenment.

Notes

Introduction

1. Paul Veyne, *Did the Greeks Believe in Their Myths?* trans. Paula Wissing (Chicago, 1988), preface.

2. English readers could, if they wished, find vernacular sketches of the pagan gods, all heavily indebted to Continental scholarship, in Cooper's *Thesaurus* (1565), updated from Sir Thomas Elyot's *Dictionary* (1543), or in an iconographical handbook without pictures published by Stephen Batman in 1577, or in Richard Lynch's adaptation of Cartari (1599), or in Abraham Fraunce's idiosyncratic rendering of the Ovidian fables (1592), or in George Sandys' commentaries on those stories (1632), or, if their taste was up to it, in Alexander Ross's lexicon of mythology (1648), laden with ingeniously Christianized allegory.

1 Euhemerism: The Medieval Tradition

1. On medieval euhemerism, see J. D. Cooke, "Euhemerism: A Mediaeval Interpretation of Classical Paganism," *Speculum* 2 (1927): 396–410; P. Alphandery, "L'Euhemerisme et les debuts de l'histoire des religions au Moyen Age," *Revue de l'histoire des religions* 119 (1934): 5–27; Jean Seznec, *The Survival of the Pagan Gods,* trans. B. F. Sessions (New York, 1953), pp. 11–26.

2. Antoine Banier, *The Mythology and Fables of the Ancients Explain'd from History* (1538), trans, anon., 4 vols. (London, 1739–40), 1:vi, vii.

3. Mircea Eliade, *Le mythe de l'éternel retour, archetypes et repetitions* (Paris, 1949), pp. 68–78.

4. Juan Luis Vives, *Opera Omnia,* 8 vols. (Benedicti Monfort, 1745), 7:3.

5. Sir Thomas Elyot, *Bibliotheca Eliotae* (London, 1545), s.v.

6. See chap. 3 in this volume.

7. See chaps. 3 and 4 in this volume.

8. This tendency is discussed in various contexts in A. B. Fergu-

son, *The Articulate Citizen and the English Renaissance* (Durham, N.C., 1965).

9. John Taylor, *The Universal Chronicle of Ralph Higden* (Oxford, 1966), p. 2. The first version of the *Polychronicon* probably dates from the 1320s.

10. Cooke, "Euhemerism."

11. *Lydgate's Troy Book,* ed. H. Bergen, Early English Texts Society, Extra Series, no. 97 (London, 1906), book 2, lines 5559–63; cf. John Gower, *Confessio Amantis,* in *Works,* ed. G. C. Macaulay, 4 vols. (Oxford, 1899–1902), book 5, lines 747–1604.

12. William Caxton, trans., *The Recuyell of the Historyes of Troye* (c. 1474), by Raoul LeFevre, ed. H. O. Sommer, 2 vols. (London, 1894), 1:249–61.

13. Ralph Higden, *Polychronicon,* ed. Churchill Babington and J. R. Lumby, Rolls Series, 9 vols. (London, 1865–86), 2:342. For the best treatment of Higden's sense of history, see J. M. Levine, *Humanism and History: Origins of Modern English Historiography* (Ithaca, 1987), pp. 32–38.

14. Higden, *Polychronicon,* 2:360–78.

15. Ibid., vol. 2, chap. 18. Unless otherwise specified, references in the following analysis are from this chapter.

16. In contrast to Isidore's "mendaciae" was "historiae," which are "resverae quae facta sunt . . . fabulae vero sunt quae nec factae sunt nec fieri possunt quia contra naturam sunt."

17. *Polychronicon,* 1:16–18; 2:422.

18. Devils, for example, might seem to change people into beasts, as in ancient legends, but the change could only be in appearance, might even be an illusion on the part of the observer, and in any case would not affect the soul. (Higden here citing Augustine.)

19. Augustine, *De civitate Dei,* 4.10.

20. *The Prologues and Epilogues of William Caxton,* ed. W. J. B. Crotch, Early English Texts Society (Oxford, 1929), p. 65.

21. Higden, *Polychronicon,* 2:ix, 281–82.

22. Ibid., 2:ix, 281–82, 364.

23. John Lydgate, *Fall of Princes,* ed. H. Bergen, 4 vols., Early English Texts Society, Extra Series, nos. 121–24 (1924–27), book 2, lines 3559–61; see also lines 5463ff. On the authorship of *Assembly of Gods,* see Early English Texts Society, Extra Series, no. 69, ed. O. L. Triggs (1896), introduction; cf. W. F. Schirmer, *John Lydgate, Ein Kulturbild aus dem 15. Jahrhundert* (Tübingen, 1952), p. 237.

24. *Assembly,* lines 1762–68.

25. *Liber Sapientia,* 14.15–21.

26. Higden, *Polychronicon,* 2:278–82; Lydgate, *Troy Book,* lines

5469–558; Gower, *Confessio,* lines 1497–604. See also Cooke, "Euhemerism."

27. References may be found in A. B. Ferguson, "Reginald Pecock and the Renaissance Sense of History," *Studies in the Renaissance* 13 (1966): 147–67, or in the same author's *Clio Unbound: Perceptions of the Social and Cultural Past in Renaissance England* (Durham, N.C., 1979), pp. 134–46.

2 A Mind Divided

1. See chap. 6 in this volume.

2. Sir Thomas Elyot, *Bibliotheca Eliotae* (London, 1545), STC 7660, s.v.

3. George Sandys, trans., *Ovid's Metamorphoses* (London, 1632), STC 18966, p. 31.

4. *The Works of Sir Walter Ralegh,* ed. Oldys and Birch (Oxford, 1829). To avoid confusion among editions, references to the *History of the World* will be made to book, chapter, and section: *History,* 1.6.4–5.

5. "Poesie" by Richard Taverner, prefaced to Abraham Fleming's translation of *A Registre of Histories . . . by Aelianus, a Romane* (London, 1576), STC 164.

6. Stephen Batman, *The Golden Booke of the Leaden Gods* (London, 1577); reprinted in The Renaissance and the Gods, no. 13, ed. Stephen Orgel (New York, 1976).

7. Ibid., introduction.

8. See, chap. 5 in this volume.

9. John Selden, commentary to Michael Drayton, *The Poly-Olbion, a Chorographical Description of Great Britain* (London, 1622), Spenser Society, New Series, nos. 1 and 3 (New York, 1970), "To the reader."

10. Ibid., book 1, lines 4, 18. See also John Selden, *Opera Omnia,* ed. David Wilkins, 6 vols. (London, 1726), vol. 2, part 2, col. 869.

11. See chap. 3 in this volume.

12. L. F. Dean, "Bodin's *Methodus* in England before 1625," *Studies in Philology* 39 (1942), 160–66.

13. John Bodin, *Method for the Easy Comprehension of History* (1566), trans. Beatrice Reynolds (New York, 1945), pp. 296–97.

14. W. L. Gundersheimer, *The Life and Works of Louis LeRoy* (Geneva, 1966), app. 1.

15. Juan Luis Vives, *Opera Omnia,* 8 vols. (Benedicti Monfort, 1745); reprint, Gregg Press (London, 1964), 8:116. Vives spent more continuous time in England than Erasmus and was in close touch with English humanists and administrators.

16. Sandys, *Ovid,* p. 26.

17. Samuel Purchas, *Purchas His Pilgrimage* (London, 1613), STC 20505, p. 68; cf. pp. 34–35.

18. Ibid., p. 71.

19. Elyot, *Bibliotheca,* proheme.

20. John Twyne, *De rebus Albionicis, Britannicis atque Anglicis* (London, 1590, but written in the main before 1550), pp. 35 and 84.

21. Vives, *De causis corruptarum artium* (1531), *Opera,* vol. 2, chaps. 4 and 5.

22. Vives, *Opera,* 8:91; see also 8:138; 6:103; 2:217, 527–28.

23. Ibid., 7:3: "Tota illa impia fabula."

24. Ibid., 8:166: "Quorum non dico historias, et res gestae, sed fabulas confictas tam libenter."

25. Ralegh, *History,* preface, pp. vi–vii. On the deification of mortals, see 5.1.4. On the part played by the devil, see 1.6.9. See also chap. 4 in this volume.

26. Ibid., 1.6.5.

27. Ibid.

28. Ibid., 1.6.1–4, 6.

29. Ibid., 2.6.4.

30. Ibid., 2.24.5.

31. Edward Herbert, Lord Cherbury, *The Ancient Religion of the Gentiles and the Causes of Their Errors Considered,* trans. William Lewis (London, 1705), p. 162. Herbert died in 1648. His *De religione gentilium* was published posthumously in 1665.

32. Ibid., p. 162; see also p. 179.

33. Ibid., p. 177.

34. Edward Stillingfleet, *Origines Sacrae* (London, 1662), pp. 24, 62.

35. John Selden, notes to *Poly-Olbion,* book 1, p. 14.

36. John Milton, *History of Britain,* in *Complete Prose Works,* vol. 5, ed. French Fogle (New Haven, 1971), pp. 4–5.

37. George Puttenham, *Arte of English Poesie,* ed. G. D. Willcock and A. Walker (Cambridge, 1936), book 2, chap. 8, p. 6; see also book 1, chap. 16. On general subject, see R. F. Jones, *The Triumph of the English Language* (Palo Alto, 1951).

38. Ibid., book 1, chap. 12.

39. Ibid.

40. Richard Wills, *De re poetica,* ed. and trans. A. D. Fowler from 1573 edition (Oxford, 1958), p. 60; Puttenham, 1.3.6; Sir Philip Sidney, *The Defence of Poesie* (1595), ed. Lewis Soens (Lincoln, Neb., 1970), p. 5. See also A. B. Ferguson, *Clio Unbound: Perceptions of the Social and Cultural Past in Renaissance England* (Durham, N.C., 1979), p. 372, for further bibliography.

41. Polydore Vergil, *De inventoribus rerum,* published in three books in 1499, with five books added in 1521.

42. B. P. Copenhaver, "The Historiography of Discovery in the Renaissance: The Source and Composition of Polydore Vergil's *De inventoribus rerum,*" *Journal of the Warburg and Courtauld Institute* 41 (1978): 192–214. On Polydore, see Denys Hay, *Polydore Vergil: Renaissance Historian and Man of Letters* (Oxford, 1952).

43. Vergil, *An Abridgement of the Notable Worke of Polidore Vergile,* trans. Thomas Langley (London, 1570), STC 24658, book 6, chap. 106, fol. 122.

44. Vives, *Opera,* 6:124.

45. Ibid., 6:16–17, also 6:8. See also ibid., 3:4–5.

46. Sir Thomas Smith, *De recta et emendata Linguae Anglicae scriptione* (Paris, 1568, but written 1542), ed. Otto Diebel (Halle, 1913), p. 9, see also pp. 2–3.

47. Sir Francis Bacon, *The Collected Works of Francis Bacon,* ed. James Spedding, R. L. Ellis, and D. D. Heath, 14 vols. (London, 1857–74), 8:512–13; cf. 8:3, 131. See also Ferguson, *Clio Unbound,* pp. 407–8.

48. Bacon, *Works,* 128.

49. Ibid. See also vol. 8, *Novum Organum,* preface and pp. 29, 108; 6:131.

50. Bacon, *Works,* 8:74; cf. 6:129.

51. See Ferguson, *Clio Unbound,* chap. 11.

52. Samuel Daniel, *Musophilus* (1599), ed. Raymond Himelick (West Lafayette, Ind., 1965), lines 803ff.

53. See chap. 3 in this volume.

54. Don Cameron Allen, *Mysteriously Meant* (Baltimore, 1970), pp. 65–66. For the parallel work of the Commentators, see Arnold Williams, *The Common Expositor: an Account of the Commentaries on Genesis 1527–1633* (Chapel Hill, 1948), pp. 208ff.

55. Ralegh, *History,* 1.6.4–5; Sandys, *Ovid,* p. 19; Alexander Ross, *Mystagogus Poeticus, or The Muses Interpreter* (London, 1648), reprinted in The Renaissance and the Gods, no. 30 (New York, 1976), introduction, and pp. 193, 197; Stillingfleet, *Origines Sacra,* book 2, chap. 5, cf. book 1, pp. 62–63; John Owen, *Theologoumena pantodapa* (Oxford, 1661), pp. 159–60. See also William Baldwin, *A Treatise of Morall Phylosopie* (London, 1546), STC 1253, sig. B, i–ii.

56. Allen, *Mysteriously Meant,* pp. 102–3.

57. Ibid., p. 70.

58. Stillingfleet, *Origines Sacrae,* p. 64.

59. Ibid., pp. 56–57; see also 68–69.

60. Ibid., 591–92.

61. Ibid., p. 8; cf. p. 64.

62. Ralegh, *History,* 1.6.5; cf. 6.1.
63. Stillingfleet, *Origines Sacrae,* pp. 8, 62, 56–57.
64. Ross, *Mystagogus Poeticus,* passim.
65. Natalis Comes [Conti], *Mythologiae,* trans. J. de Montlyard, ed. J. Baudoin (1597), reprint of 1627 edition in The Renaissance and the Gods, no. 26 (New York, 1976), p. 5.
66. Jean Seznec, *The Survival of the Pagan Gods,* trans. B. F. Sessions (New York, 1953), p. 256.
67. Comes [Conti], *Mythologiae,* book 2, chap. 2.
68. Abraham Fraunce, *The Third Part of the Countesse of Pembrokes Yuychurch,* ed. Gerald Snare (Northridge, Calif., 1975), comment on First Tale.
69. Ibid., p. 19.
70. Roger Howell, *Sir Philip Sidney, the Shepherd Knight* (Boston, 1968), p. 25.
71. See chap. 6 in this volume.
72. Bacon, *Works,* 8:92.
73. Ibid., 13:76; 8:443.
74. Paolo Rossi, *Francis Bacon: From Magic to Science* (Chicago, 1968), chap. 3. See also Barbara Garman Garner, "Francis Bacon, Natalis Comes and the Mythological Tradition," *Journal of Warburg and Courtauld Institutes,* 33 (1970), 264–91.
75. Bacon, *Works,* 8:350.
76. Thomas Blackwell, *Letters Concerning Mythology* (London, 1748), reprinted in The Renaissance and the Gods, no. 42 (New York, 1976).
77. See chap. 5 in this volume.
78. See D. C. Allen, *The Legend of Noah: Renaissance Rationalism in Art, Science and Letters* (Urbana, Ill., 1963).
79. Williams, *The Common Expositor,* chap. 3.
80. Comes [Conti], book 1, p. 544; Vives, *Opera,* 8:116; Bacon, *Works,* 13:77; Sandys, *Ovid,* p. 26; Stillingfleet, *Origines Sacrae,* pp. 8, 62, 65–67.
81. Palaephatus, *De incredibilibus,* excerpts in Hyginus, *Fabularum liber* (Basle, 1535), reprinted in The Renaissance and the Gods, no. 6 (New York, 1976), p. 116.
82. Ibid., pp. 120–21.
83. The book went through twenty editions in Latin before 1788; it appeared in Italian by 1545 and in French in 1558. Allen, *Mysteriously Meant,* p. 58.
84. Sir Thomas Browne, *Pseudodoxia epidemica, or Enquiries into very many received Tenents [sic] and commonly presumed Truth* (London, 1646), book 1, p. 6. See also C. W. Lemmi, *The Classical Deities in Bacon* (Baltimore, 1933), p. 28. On Palaephatus, see Paul Veyne, *Did the*

Greeks Believe in Their Myths? trans. Paula Wissing (Chicago, 1988), pp. 67–70.

85. Plato, *Works,* ed. and trans. B. Jowett, 4 vols. (New York, n.d.), 3:382.

86. Bacon, *Works,* 6:184–86.

87. Sandys, *Ovid,* preface; cf. Henry Reynolds, *Mythomystes* (London, 1632), STC 20939, pp. 64ff.

88. Bacon, *Works,* 13:78.

3 The Age of Myth

1. See chap. 4.

2. Juan Luis Vives, *Opera Omnia,* 8 vols. (Benedicti Monfort, 1745), 6:103.

3. Francis Bacon, *The Collected Works,* 14 vols. (London, 1857–74), 13:75.

4. Reginald Pecock, *The Folewer to the Donet,* ed. E. V. Hitchcock, Early English Texts Society, Original Series, 164 (London, 1924), p. 80. See also chap. 1, n. 12 in this volume.

5. E.g., Thomas Lydiat, Robert Pont, Thomas Pye, Henry Isaacson, Ludowick Lloyd, and John More. John Selden tackled the problem of basic chronology in his *De Dis Syris,* in *Opera Omnia,* ed. David Wilkins (London, 1726), vol. 2, and Edward Stillingfleet in *Origines Sacrae* (London, 1662). On William Harrison's manuscript chronology, see J. G. R. Parry, *A Protestant Vision* (Cambridge, 1987). See also Frank Manuel, *The Eighteenth Century Confronts the Gods* (New York, 1967), pp. 112, 118; and A. T. Grafton, "Scaliger and Historical Chronology," *History and Theory* 14 (1923), 156–85.

6. Parry, *Protestant Vision,* passim; Stuart Piggott, *Ancient Britons and the Antiquarian Imagination* (London, 1989), chap. 2.

7. Ludowick Lloyd, *The Consent of Time* (London, 1590), STC 16619, epistle.

8. An especially full and late appeal to Varro's authority may be found in Antoine Banier, *The Mythology and Fables of the Ancients Explained from History,* 4 vols. (London, 1739–40), 1:61–64. Cf. William Camden, *Britannia,* trans. Philemon Holland (London, 1610), 1:lxxlii.

9. Vives, *Opera,* vol. 2; 6:103; cf. 3:3.

10. Ibid., 8:217.

11. Camden, *Britannia,* 1:lxxiii.

12. D. R. Woolf, *The Idea of History in Early Stuart England* (Toronto, 1990), pp. 208 and 211.

13. George Sandys, trans., *Ovid's Metamorphoses* (London, 1632), preface.

14. Richard Wills, *De re poetica* (Oxford, 1958), p. 60.

15. Walter Ralegh, *History,* 1.6.1, in *Works,* ed. Oldys and Birch (Oxford, 1829).

16. Ibid., 1.6.4.

17. Don Cameron Allen, *Mysteriously Meant* (Baltimore, 1970), p. 71.

18. Stillingfleet, *Origines Sacrae,* p. 14.

19. Ibid., pp. 56ff.

20. Ibid., p. 597.

21. The following argument is contained in ibid., pp. 57–61.

22. Ibid., pp. 585–86.

23. Ibid., p. 593. "Bochartus," he says, cites fourteen parallels with Saturn.

24. Ibid., p. 587.

25. Ibid., p. 589.

26. Ibid., p. 587.

27. Ibid., p. 588.

28. R. F. Jones, *Ancients and Moderns* (Berkeley, 1965), see especially chaps. 2 and 3.

29. See A. B. Ferguson, *Clio Unbound* (Durham, N.C., 1979).

30. R. T. Carroll, *The Common-sense Philosophy of Religion of Edward Stillingfleet* (The Hague, 1975).

31. Bacon, *Works,* 13:75.

32. Ibid., 13:77–78.

33. Ibid., 12:121. It has been argued that Bacon's famous "idols"—of the tribe, the cave, the market place and the theatre—represent successive stages of the development of mankind; see Woolf, *Idea of History,* pp. 145–46. Cf. F. J. Levy, *Tudor Historical Thought* (San Marino, Calif., 1967), pp. 254–55; Ferguson, *Clio Unbound,* pp. 46–48.

34. Bacon, *Works,* 13:80; 8:442. See also Paolo Rossi, *Francis Bacon: From Magic to Science* (Chicago, 1968), pp. 87, 127.

35. D. J. Gordon, *The Renaissance Imagination,* ed. Stephen Orgel (Berkeley, 1975), pp. 16–17. See also, Allen, *Mysteriously Meant,* chap. 5.

36. T. C. Singer, "Hieroglyphs, Real Characters, and the Idea of Natural Language in English Seventeenth-Century Thought," *Journal of the History of Ideas* 50 (1989), 49–70.

37. Sir John Price, *Historia Brytannicae defensio* (London, 1573), STC 20309, p. 18.

38. Stillingfleet, *Origines Sacrae,* pp. 18–19.

39. Bacon, *Works,* 6:204.

40. Ibid.; also 13:80. Cf. Price, *Defensio,* p. 18.

41. Samuel Daniel, trans., *The Worthy Tract of Paulus Iovius* (London, 1585), preface.

42. On Augustine, see George Boas, *Essays on Primitivism and Related Ideas in the Middle Ages* (New York, 1966), pp. 47, 177–80.

43. E.g., John Colet, *Letters to Radulphus on the Mosaic Account of the Creation,* in *Opuscula Quaedam Theologica,* trans. J. H. Lupton (London, 1876), p. 28 (Latin text, p. 182); Vives, *Opera,* 8:17, 105, 182.

44. Bacon, *Works,* 6:129; 8:116; cf. Ralegh, *History,* 6.1.4.

45. See chap. 4 of this volume.

46. Richard Eden, trans., *The Decades of the Newe Worlde,* by Peter Martyr (London, 1555), reprinted in *The First Three English Books on America,* ed. Edward Arber (Westminster, 1895), p. 99. This is one of the many marginal commentaries he made to the translation.

47. Vives, *Opera,* 7:217.

48. Margaret T. Hodgen, *Early Anthropology in the Sixteenth and Seventeenth Centuries* (Philadelphia, 1964), pp. 330ff.

49. The idea was virtually a commonplace. The following are representative examples in English letters: Thomas Wilson, *The Art of Rhetorique* (1560), ed. G. H. Mair (London, 1909), pp. 195ff.; Arthur Golding, *The Fyrst Fowr Bookes of P. Ovidius Nasos . . . Metamorphosis* (London, 1565), STC 18955, preface; Sandys, *Ovid,* preface; Ralegh, *History,* 2.6.4; Edmund Spenser, *The Faerie Queene,* book 6, prologue; and, of course, Bacon's *De Sapientia Veterum, Works,* vol. 13, preface.

50. Rossi, *Bacon,* pp. 127–28; see chap. 3 passim.

51. Bacon, *Works,* 8:154.

52. See chap. 2 of this volume.

53. Bacon, *Works,* 13:76; cf. 8:443.

54. Ibid., 13:155–56; See also Achsah Guibbory, *The Map of Time* (Urbana, Ill., 1986), p. 54.

55. Bacon, *Works,* 13:78–79.

56. For an exhaustive analysis of Bacon's debt, in particular, to Conti's *Mythologiae,* but one that largely misses the point of his use of the fables, see C. W. Lemmi, *The Classical Deities in Bacon* (Baltimore, 1933).

57. Bacon, *Works,* 8:403.

4 A Secular Alternative

1. Exact references may be found conveniently in A. O. Lovejoy and George Boas, *Primitivism and Related Ideas in Antiquity* (Baltimore, 1915). See also Boas, *Essays on Primitivism and Related Ideas in the Middle Ages* (New York, 1966), especially pp. 175–205.

2. The following list is not meant to be exhaustive but to give some idea of the variety of writings in which the cave myth appeared: Thomas Cranmer, *Miscallaneous Writings,* Parker Society (London, 1846), pp. 118–19; Richard Eden, trans., *The Decades of the Newe Worlde* (London, 1555), reprinted in *The First Three English Books on America,* ed. Edward Arber (Westminster, 1895), preface, p. 57; Sir Thomas Elyot, *The Boke Named the Gouernour* (London, 1531), ed. H. H. S. Croft, 2 vols. (London, 1880), 1:117; D. Erasmus, *Dulce bellum inexpertis* (1513–15), ed. and trans. J. W. Mackail, in *Erasmus against War* (Boston, 1907), pp. 18–23; Abraham Fraunce, *The Third Part of the Countesse of Pembrokes Yuychurch,* ed. Gerald Snare (Northridge, Calif., 1975), p. 19; Peter Heylyn, *Cosmography* (first printed, 1652, enlarged, London, 1674), pp. 3–4; Thomas Hobbes, *Leviathan,* ed. W. G. Pogson Smith (Oxford, 1958), pp. 96–98; Richard Puttenham, *The Arte of English Poesie* (1589), ed. G. D. Willcock and A. Walker (Cambridge, 1936), book 1, pp. iii, 6; Robert Recorde, *The Grounde of Artes* (London, 1542), STC 20798, preface; Sir Thomas Smith, *De recta et emendata linguae Anglicae scriptione, Dialogus* (1568), ed. Otto Deibel (Halle, 1913), pp. 2–3; John Twyne, *De rebus Britannicis, Albionicis atque Anglicis* (London, 1590), STC 24407, pp. 63–65; Juan Luis Vives, *Opera Omnia,* 8 vols. (Benedicti Monfort, 1745), reprint, Gregg Press (London, 1964), 8:75–76; see also *Vives: On Education,* ed. and trans. Foster Watson (Cambridge, 1913), p. 12; Thomas Wilson, *The Arte of Rhetorique* (1560), ed. L. H. Mair (London, 1909), preface; Thomas Starkey, *Dialogue between Pole and Lupset,* ed. T. F. Mayer, Camden Society, Fourth Series, vol. 37 (London, 1989), pp. 35–36, also pp. 5 and 11. Conventional use of the cave myth by historians is exemplified in Ralph Higden, *Polychronicon* (London, 1865–86), book 2, p. 364, and Walter Ralegh, *History,* 5.1.4, 2.6.4, in *Works,* ed. Oldys and Birch (Oxford, 1829). The cave myth is implicit in William Camden's *Britannia* (London, 1610), pp. 4–5, and John Speed's *History of Great Britain* (London, 1611), pp. 166–70—in both cases implied in references to the early Britons.

3. Starkey's *Dialogue* was written sometime between 1529 and 1532 (p. x) but was not published until the nineteenth century. It was apparently circulated effectively in court circles, however.

4. Starkey, *Dialogue,* pp. 35–36; see also pp. 5 and 11.

5. Ibid., p. 2.

6. Ibid., p. 19.

7. A. B. Ferguson, *Clio Unbound* (Durham, N.C., 1979), chap. 13.

8. Starkey, *Dialogue,* p. 137.

9. Ralegh, *History,* 2.6.4.

10. See chap. 5 in this volume.

11. Nathanael Carpenter, *Geography Delineated Forth in Two Books*

(London, 1625), STC 4676 II, sig. Nn; cf. Peter Heylyn, *Microcosmus* (London, 1621), p. 252.

12. Sir Thomas Smith, *De Republica Anglorum,* ed. L. Alston (Cambridge, 1906), book 1, chaps. 11–14.

13. Richard Hooker, *Of the Laws of Ecclesiastical Polity,* ed. George Edelen et al., 4 vols. (Cambridge, Mass., 1977–83), e.g.,1.6.1–4, 1.10.2–5.

14. See chap. 3 in this volume.

15. First published in 1520, translated by William Prat in 1550 and by William Watreman in 1555, and incorporated by Thomas Lanquet in his *Epitome of Chronicles* (London, 1549), STC 15217.

16. *Erasmus against War.*

17. Vives, *On Education,* pp. 12ff. See also Ferguson, *Clio Unbound,* p. 363.

18. Louis LeRoy, *De la vicissitude ou variété des choses en l'univers* (1575), trans. Robert Ashley, *Of the Interchangeable Course, or Variety of Things in the World* (London, 1594), STC 15488. In his preface to the translation, Ashley wrote that he undertook it because of "the great liking" he noticed "generally conceived of the work." See also W. L. Gundersheimer, *The Life and Works of Louis LeRoy* (Geneva, 1966), app. 1, for LeRoy's popularity in England.

19. Aristotle, *Politics,* book 1, chap. 2.

20. LeRoy, *Interchangeable Course,* fol. 29ʳ.

21. Vives, *Opera,* 6:1, 3. See also pp. 6 and 20; cf. Hooker, *Laws,* 1.5.3.

22. Vives, *Opera,* 6:8ff.

23. See, for example, excerpts from Lucretius, Cicero, and Vitruvius in Lovejoy and Boas, *Primitivism,* pp. 229, 245, and 375 respectively.

24. Vives, *On Education,* p. 114; see also pp. 12ff.; cf. *Opera,* 8:75–76. Vives vacillated between a referential and a relational semantics. Richard Waswo, *Language and Meaning in the Renaissance* (Princeton, 1987), pp. 113–33. See also Lanquet, *Epitome,* sigs. Aii–Bi.

25. Puttenham, *Arte,* book 2, p. 4.

26. William Webbe, *A Discourse of English Poetrie* (London, 1586), pp. 21–22.

27. Eden, *Decades,* p. xliii; see also Vives, *Opera,* 8:77.

28. Puttenham, *Arte,* book 2, p. 4.

29. Jean Bodin, *Method for the Easy Comprehension of History,* trans. Beatrice Reynolds (New York, 1945), p. 303; cf. pp. 334–35. See also L. F. Dean, "Bodin's *Methodus* in England before 1625," *Studies in Philology* 39 (1942): 160–66.

30. Genesis 4:17–22.

31. Arnold Williams, *The Common Expositor: An Account of the Com-

mentaries on Genesis 1527–1633 (Chapel Hill, N.C., 1948), chap. 2. An important English example is Andrew Willet, *Hexapla in Genesin, That is, a Sixfold Commentary upon Genesis* (London, 1608), STC 25683a.

32. Wilson, *Arte of Rhetorique,* preface.

33. Heylyn, *Cosmography,* pp. 3–4.

34. Hooker, *Laws,* 1.10.2–5.

35. On Boemus's influence, see Margaret T. Hodgen, *Early Anthropology in the Sixteenth and Seventeenth Centuries* (Philadelphia, 1964), pp. 32–33.

36. Wyllyam Prat, *Description of the Country of Affrique* (London, 1554), STC 191, preface; see also chaps. 1 and 2 passim. This is a translation of a French version of Johann Boemus's *Omnium gentium mores* (1536). Cf. another translation by William Watreman, *The Fardle of Facions* (London, 1555), STC 3197, and Thomas Lanquet, *Epitome,* fols. 1–5.

37. Lucretius, *De rerum naturae,* book 5, lines 780ff.

38. Edward Stillingfleet, *Origines Sacrae* (London, 1662), p. 447.

39. Ralegh, *History,* 2.11.3, cf. 1.1.15 and preface.

40. LeRoy, *Interchangeable Course,* fols. 27^{r}–31^{v}.

41. See chap. 2 in this volume.

42. *The Politics of Aristotle,* ed. and trans. Ernest Barker (New York, 1962), p. 104.

43. LeRoy, *Interchangeable Course,* fols. 27^{r}–31^{v}. For other examples, see William Baldwin, *A Treatise of Morall Phylosophie* (London, 1547), STC 1253, fols. 11–13; Ralegh, *History,* 1.9.1; Lanquet, *Epitome,* fol. 4^{v}; Vives, *Opera,* 6:8ff.

44. See Lovejoy and Boas, *Primitivism,* for examples.

45. Williams, *Common Expositor,* p. 108.

46. Starkey, *Dialogue,* p. 6.

47. See Ferguson, *Clio Unbound,* chap. 11.

48. Smith, *De recta,* pp. 2–3.

49. Bodin, *Method,* pp. 296–98.

50. See R. F. Jones, *Ancients and Moderns* (Berkeley, 1965), chap. 2.

51. Robert Nisbet, *History of the Idea of Progress* (New York, 1930), p. 101; cf. Achsah Guibbory, *The Map of Time* (Urbana, Ill., 1986), p. 18.

52. See chap. 2 in this volume.

53. Watreman, *Fardle of Facions,* preface.

54. Hooker, *Laws,* 1.10.3, cf. 1.8.7.

55. Ibid., 1.6.1, cf. 1.10.2; cf. Vives, *On Education,* p. 20.

56. Eden, *Decades,* preface, p. 57.

57. See chap. 3 in this volume. On the interest taken in the Irish as primitives, see D. B. Quinn, *The Elizabethans and the Irish* (Ithaca, 1966), chap. 4.

58. Hodgen, *Early Anthropology,* pp. 449ff.

59. Eden, *Decades,* p. 146. On Elizabethan perceptions, see R. R. Cawley, *Unpathed Waters: Studies in the Influence of the Voyages on Elizabethan Literature* (Princeton, 1940); R. H. Pearce, *The Savage of America* (Baltimore, 1953); Louis B. Wright, *The Elizabethan America* (Cambridge, Mass., 1965).

60. Ralegh, *History,* 5.1.4. See Hodgen, *Early Anthropology,* chap. 9.

61. Puttenham, *Arte,* book 1, p. 10. Sir John Davies could not help contrasting the elaborate legal systems of his own day with the simplicity of primitive law among the Roman people when they were "little better than shepherds and herdsmen" or among the savages of the New World: *Irish Reports* (1615) (London, 1674), preface, fol. 5.

62. LeRoy, *Interchangeable Course,* fol. 27^{v}.

63. Margaret Hodgen's phrase, *Early Anthropology,* p. 34.

64. See Richard Bernheimer, *Wild Men in the Middle Ages* (New York, 1970), and Donald Cheney, *Spenser's Image of Nature: Wild Men and Shepherds in "The Faerie Queene"* (New Haven, 1966).

65. Twyne, *De rebus,* pp. 8, 56–58, 64, 87, 91.

66. Speed, *History,* pp. 166–70.

67. Quentin Skinner, *The Foundations of Modern Political Thought,* 2 vols. (Cambridge, 1978), vol. 2, chap. 5, especially 153.

68. See, in general, Hooker, *Laws,* 1.10.1–5.

69. Ibid., 1.6.1; cf. 1.10.2.

70. Ibid., 1.10.3.

71. Ibid., 1.8.7.

72. Thomas Hobbes, *Leviathan,* ed. W. G. Pogson Smith (Oxford, 1958), p. 97.

73. The literature on this point is extensive. For a brief review of the main points of view, see G. J. Schochet, *Patriarchalism and Political Thought* (Oxford, 1975), chap. 12; W. R. Lund, "The Historical and 'Politicall' Origins of Civil Society: Hobbes on Presumption and Certainty," *History of Political Thought* 9 (1988): 223–35.

74. Hobbes, *Leviathan,* pp. 96–97.

75. See Camden, *Brittania,* pp. 4–5.

76. *The English Works of Thomas Hobbes,* ed. William Molesworth, 11 vols. (London, 1839–45), 4:75.

5 The British History: The Problem of Legend

1. A. B. Ferguson, *The Chivalric Ideal in Renaissance England* (Durham, N.C., 1986), pp. 136–38; Sydney Anglo, "The British History in Early Tudor Propaganda," *Bulletin of the John Rylands Library*

44 (1961): 17–18; T. D. Kendrick, *British Antiquity* (London, 1950), pp. 42–43.

2. Sydney Anglo, *Spectacle, Pageantry and Early Tudor Policy* (Oxford, 1969).

3. John Rastell, *The Pastime of People* (London, 1529), ed. T. F. Dibdin (London, 1811), pp. 3–6.

4. John Bale, *The Laboryouse Journey and Serche of Johan Leylande for England's Antiquities,* in *The Itinerary of John Leland,* ed. Lucy Toulman Smith, 5 vols. (Carbondale, Ill., 1964), 1:xxxvii–xliii, preface.

5. Bale was, in a sense, author of the first history of English literature: *Scriptorum illustrium majoris Britanniae* (Basel, 1557–59).

6. On the Samothes legend, see Kendrick, *British Antiquity,* pp. 72–76.

7. Like Bale, William Harrison, whose *Description of Britain* is prefixed to Holinshed's *Chronicle,* may have found Samothes more congenial than Brutus to his radically Protestant view of history; see G. J. R. Parry, *A Protestant Vision* (Cambridge, 1987), p. 73.

8. D. R. Woolf, *The Idea of History in Early Stuart England* (Toronto, 1990), pp. 13–23.

9. On Leland, see n. 4 above; John Twyne, *De rebus Albionicis, Britannicis atque Anglicis* (London, 1590, but written before the midcentury).

10. Rastell, *Pastime,* pp. 3–6; Twyne, *De rebus,* p. 97.

11. *Polydore Vergil's English History* (from an early translation), ed. Sir Henry Ellis, Camden Society, no. 36 (London, 1846), p. 29.

12. John Leland, *Assertio inclytissimi Arturii regis Britanniae* (London, 1544), trans. Richard Robinson (1582), in *The Famous Historie of Chinon of England by Christopher Middleton,* ed. W. E. Mead, Early English Texts Society, Original Series, no. 165 (London, 1925).

13. Geoffrey of Monmouth, *Historia regum Britanniae,* ed. C. W. Dunn (New York, 1958), dedicatory epistle.

14. William of Newburgh, *Historia rerum Anglicarum,* ed. Richard Howlett, Rolls Series, no. 82 (London, 1884), pp. 10–18. See Kendrick, *British Antiquity,* pp. 12–13.

15. See A. B. Ferguson, *The Articulate Citizen and the English Renaissance* (Durham, N.C., 1965), part 1.

16. Quoted by Laura Keeler, *Geoffrey of Monmouth and the Chronicles* (Princeton, 1957), pp. 82–83. See also Kendrick, *British Antiquity,* pp. 34–35.

17. Ralph Higden, *Polychronicon,* ed. Churchill Babington and J. R. Lumby, Rolls Series, 9 vols. (London, 1885–86), 5:325–37.

18. J. M. Levine, *Humanism and History: Origins of Modern English Historiography* (Ithaca, 1987), pp. 44–45.

19. Kendrick, *British Antiquity,* p. 35.

20. Rastell, *Pastime,* pp. 3–6, 107–8.

21. Kendrick has called Twyne "one of the most original antiquaries of the sixteenth century." *British Antiquity,* p. 105. A much-needed translation of this work is in the process of completion.

22. Twyne refers to Vives repeatedly and with all appearance of intimacy: *De rebus,* pp. 6–7, 41–42, 44, 131.

23. Sir Walter Ralegh, *History,* 2.21.6, in *Works,* ed. Oldys and Birch (Oxford, 1829).

24. Twyne, *De rebus,* pp. 39, 66–67, 120. Cf. Vives, *De ratione dicendi,* in *Opera,* 2:213, 265.

25. Twyne, *De rebus,* pp. 80–83, 91, 143–44.

26. Ibid., pp. 7–9, 15–31, 98–107. After the publication of his book in 1590, Twyne's theory appears to have attracted some attention among later antiquarian scholars, including Lambarde, Norder, Verstegen, and Harrison. Camden was noncommittal.

27. Twyne, *De rebus,* pp. 63, 64. See chap. 4 in this volume.

28. William Camden, *Britannia,* trans. Philemon Holland (London, 1610), pp. 4–5. *Britannia* was first published in 1586; an enlarged edition appeared in 1606.

29. Ibid., pp. 6–9.

30. Ibid., pp. 33–34.

31. Ibid., p. 9.

32. Ibid., p. 16.

33. F. J. Levy, *Tudor Historical Thought* (San Marino, Calif., 1967), pp. 131–33.

34. For a summary of this argument, see Kendrick, *British Antiquity,* pp. 87ff.

35. Sir John Price, *Historiae Britannicae defensio* (London, 1573), STC 20309, preface. The book is dedicated to Edward VI and was mostly written in 1545. Cf. Humphrey Lhuyd, *The Breviary of Britayne,* trans. Thomas Twyne (London, 1573), STC 16636, fols. 2–7.

36. Price, *Defensio,* pp. 8, 10.

37. Ibid., pp. 13–14, 17.

38. Lhuyd, *Breviary,* fols. 42–43.

39. Ibid., fols. 1–4.

40. Kendrick, *British Antiquity,* p. 65.

41. See ibid., 85–87.

42. On the attitude toward things Roman, see, for example, Leland, *Assertio,* p. 83.

43. Ibid., p. 54.

44. T. D. Kendrick, foreword to Leland, *Itinerary.*

45. Leland, *Assertio,* pp. 54–60.

46. Rastell, *Pastime,* p. 107.

47. Camden, *Britannia,* p. 265.

48. Leland, *Assertio,* pp. 54, 27.

49. William Warner, *Albion's England* (1586); Michael Drayton, *Poly-Olbion* (1622).

50. Levine, *Humanism,* p. 52.

51. John Selden, commentary to Michael Drayton, *The Poly-Olbion, a Chorographical Description of Great Britain* (London, 1622), Spenser Society, New Series, no. 1 (New York, 1970), book 1, pp. 69–70.

52. Price, *Defensio,* p. 22.

53. Kendrick, *British Antiquity,* p. 43; see also, p. 37.

54. Quoted in Edwin A. Greenlaw, *Studies in Spenser's Historical Allegory* (Baltimore, 1932), pp. 155–56.

55. Kendrick, *British Antiquity,* pp. 114–20.

56. Rastell, *Pastime,* p. 7.

57. Selden, commentary to *Poly-Olbion,* book 1, p. 17. See also Selden's edition of Fortescue's *De Laudibus Legum Angliae* (1616), trans. Robert Mulcaster (London, 1672), notes to chap. 17.

58. Kendrick, *British Antiquity,* pp. 109–10.

59. Camden, *Britannia,* trans. and ed. Richard Gough, 3 vols. (London, 1789), 1:xxi.

60. Samuel Daniel, *Musophilus, in Poems and a Defence of Rhyme,* ed. A. C. Sprague (Cambridge, Mass., 1930), lines 337ff.

61. John Clapham, *The Historie of England* (London, 1602), STC 5347, preface.

62. *The Reports of Sir Edward Coke,* ed. J. H. Thomson and J. F. Fraser (London, 1826), vol. 2, preface.

63. George Salter, *Of the Antient Lawes of Greate Britaine* (London, 1605), STC 27635. Not surprisingly, Salter leaned heavily on the work of Sir John Price.

64. Camden, *Britannia* (London, 1610), p. 28.

65. Selden, commentary to *Poly-Olbion,* book 1, p. 167.

66. Ibid. Reference here is to the "stethus."

67. Ibid., book 1, p. 17.

68. *The Works of Edmund Spenser,* ed. Edwin A. Greenlaw et al., 11 vols. (Baltimore, 1932–57), 10:90.

69. John Milton, *The History of Britain,* in *Complete Prose Works,* vol. 5, ed. French Fogle (New Haven, 1971), p. 3. See also Barbara J. Shapiro, *Probability and Certainty in Seventeenth-Century England* (Princeton, 1983), p. 146.

70. Price, *Defensio,* pp. 7, 13–14.

71. Camden, *Britannia* (London, 1789), 1:li–lv.

72. Selden, commentary to *Poly-Olbion,* "To the reader"; see also book 1, pp. 17, 69, 70, and *Opera Omnia,* 2:365.

73. Edmund Spenser, *A View of the Present State of Ireland,* ed. W. L. Renwick (Oxford, 1970), pp. 39–40. See chap. 6 in this volume.

74. Twyne, *De rebus,* p. 35. Twyne's attitude toward Homer no doubt reflected that of Vives in the latter's earlier years before he had come to appreciate Homer strictly as a poet. See Vives, *Opera,* 7:106–7, and C. G. Norena, *Juan Luis Vives* (The Hague, 1970), pp. 44–66.

75. Drayton, *Poly-Olbion,* book 1, pp. 162–63.

76. William Harrison, *An Historical Description of the Island of Britain,* prefixed to Ralph Holinshed, *Chronicles,* ed. Sir Henry Ellis, 6 vols. (London, 1807–8), 1:34–37.

77. Price, *Defensio,* p. 18: "Hinc Hyeroglyphicae figurae ante repertas literas hinc est quod nonnulli maiorum suorum res memorabiles . . . vel saxis et cautibus ipsis insculpere curaverint. Hinc Poetarum fabulae."

78. Camden, *Britannia* (London, 1789), 1:lxxiii. See chap. 3 in this volume for more on Varro.

79. Polydore Vergil, *English History,* book 1, p. 31.

80. Twyne, *De rebus,* pp. 91–92.

81. Ibid., pp. 91, 161.

82. Selden, commentary to *Poly-Olbion,* book 1, p. 16.

6 A Digression on Giants

1. See above. Except where specific reference is needed, material already covered in previous chapters will not be reannotated.

2. Walter Stephens, *Giants in Those Days* (Lincoln, Nebr. and London, 1989), p. 209.

3. On the history of perceptions of giants, see ibid.

4. Sir Walter Ralegh, *History,* 1.5.8, in *Works,* ed. Oldys and Birch (Oxford, 1829); Ralph Higden, *Polychronicon* (London, 1865–86), 2:230; Samuel Purchas, *Purchas His Pilgrimage* (London, 1513), pp. 32–33.

5. John Twyne, *De Rebus Albionicis, Britannicis atque Anglicis* (London, 1590, but written before the midcentury).

6. Ibid., p. 75.

7. Ibid., pp. 60, 63–64.

8. Ibid., pp. 59–63.

9. Ibid., p. 90.

10. Ibid., pp. 63–64. On the "cave myth," see chap. 4 in this volume.

11. Twyne, *De rebus,* p. 64.

12. See chap. 2 in this volume.

13. John Norden, *Speculum Britanniae* (London, 1593), STC 18635, p. 4.

14. Alexander Ross, *Mystagogus Poeticus* (London, 1648), reprinted in The Renaissance and the Gods, no. 30 (New York, 1976), pp. 37–38.

15. Goropius was also known as Johan van Gorp. The *Gigantomachia* appeared in his *Origines Antwerpianae* (Antwerp, 1569), pp. 137–226.

16. Arnold Williams, *The Common Expositor: An Account of the Commentaries on Genesis 1527–1633* (Chapel Hill, N.C., 1948), p. 152.

17. William Harrison, *Description of Britain,* in Holinshed, *Chronicles,* ed. Henry Ellis (London, 1807–8), vol. 1, chap. 9; Ralegh, *History,* 1.5.8.

18. Ibid., pp. 14–15.

19. John Selden, commentary to Michael Drayton, *The Poly-Olbion* (London, 1622), book 1, pp. 20–21.

20. Ibid., pp. 49–50.

21. Inigo Jones, *The Most Notable Antiquity of Great Britain Vulgarly Called Stonehenge* (London, 1655), pp. 17–18. A facsimile edition has been published by Scolar Press (Menston, 1973).

22. Thomas Molyneux, *Philosophical Transactions of the Royal Society* 20 (1700–1701): 507–8.

23. Stuart Piggott, *Ancient Britons and the Antiquarian Imagination* (London, 1989), p. 48.

7 "Poesie Historical"

1. Plato, *The Republic,* in *The Works of Plato,* ed. and trans. B. Jowett (New York, n.d.), books 3 and 10.

2. Ibid., introduction, p. 49.

3. William Nelson, *Fact or Fiction: The Dilemma of the Renaissance Storyteller* (Cambridge, Mass., 1973), introduction.

4. *M. Tulii Ciceronii Opera,* 8 vols. (Turin, 1945), 1:100.

5. Aristotle, *On the Art of Poetry,* trans. S. H. Butcher, ed. M. C. Nahm (New York, 1950), p. 3; see also Michael McKeon, *The Origins of the English Novel* (Baltimore, 1987), pp. 53–54.

6. Erich Auerbach, *Mimesis: the Representation of Reality in Western Literature,* trans. W. R. Trask (Princeton, 1953), pp. 7–14.

7. Arnold Sikes, *The Anthropology of the Greeks* (London, 1914), pp. 2–3.

8. See n. 23 to this chapter.

9. Juan Luis Vives, *De Causis Corruptarum Artium* (1531), part 2, chaps. 4–5, in *Opera Omnia,* 8 vols. (Benedicti Monfort, 1745), vol. 6. On the changes in Vives' literary taste, see C. G. Norena, *Juan Luis Vives* (The Hague, 1970), p. 60.

10. Vives, *Veritas fucata, sive de licentia poetica,* in *Opera,* 2:517–31; cf. *De Causis,* pp. 94 and 103.

11. J. E. Spingarn, *A History of Literary Criticism in the Renaissance* (New York, 1899), p. 13.

12. For the material contained in this paragraph, see McKeon, *Origins,* chap. 1.

13. Judith H. Anderson, *Biographical Truth: The Representation of Historical Persons in Tudor-Stuart Writing* (New Haven, 1984).

14. See Paul Descharme, *La critique des traditions religieuses chez les grecs* (Paris, 1904), chap. 12.

15. Vives, *Opera,* 2:47, 219; 6:93–94.

16. Edmund Spenser, *Tears of the Muses,* lines 461–62, *Ruins of Time,* lines 421–27, in *The Minor Poems of Edmund Spenser,* ed. E. De Selincourt (Oxford, 1910).

17. Thomas Heywood, *The Golden Age* (1611), in *The Dramatic Works of Thomas Heywood,* 6 vols. (London, 1874), 3:77, 88.

18. See chap. 1 in this volume.

19. See chap. 3 in this volume.

20. E.g., Stephen Gosson, *The Schoole of Abuse* (London, 1579), STC 12097. See also Russell Fraser, *The War against Poetry* (Princeton, 1970).

21. Edmund Spenser, *A View of the Present State of Ireland,* ed. W. L. Renwick (Oxford, 1970), pp. 39–40.

22. William Harrison, *Description of Britain,* in Holinshed, *Chronicles* ed. Henry Ellis (London, 1807–8), p. 37.

23. John Colet, *Letters to Radulphus on the Mosaic Account of the Creation,* ed. and trans. J. H. Lupton (London, 1876), p. 14; see also, pp. 8–9.

24. George Sandys, trans., *Ovid's Metamorphoses* (London, 1632), pp. 19, 26.

25. George Puttenham published his *Arte of English Poesie* in 1589, but it embodied materials that date back some thirty years. On the subject of historical poetry, see Andrew Fichter, *Poets Historical: Dynastic Epic in the Renaissance* (New Haven, 1982).

26. Puttenham, *Arte,* part 1, chaps. 3–4.

27. Ibid., part 1, chap. 19.

28. Aristotle, *Art of Poetry,* p. 13.

29. Sir Philip Sidney, *The Defence of Poesie,* ed. Lewis Soens (Lincoln, 1970), p. 22.

30. Ibid., p. 19.

31. Ibid., pp. 17–18.

32. Ibid., p. 20; see also p. 6. Cf. Sir Walter Ralegh, *History,* 2.21.6, in *Works,* ed. Oldys and Birch (Oxford, 1829).

33. Sidney, *Defence,* pp. 17–18.

34. Ibid., pp. 55–56; see also pp. 4–5.

35. Ibid., p. 9.

36. Fichter, *Poets Historical,* p. 2.

37. *The Poetical Works of Edmund Spenser,* ed. J. C. Smith and E. De Selincourt (London, 1965), p. 408.

38. Spenser, *Faerie Queene,* book 2, proem; see also 2.9.59–60.

39. Spenser, *View,* in *The Works of Edmund Spenser: A Variorum Edition,* ed. E. A. Greenlaw et al., 11 vols. (Baltimore, 1932–57), 10:82, and apparatus, line 1152. On this aspect of Spenser's thought, see Judith H. Anderson, "The Antiquities of Fairland and Ireland," *Journal of English and Germanic Philology* 86 (1987): 199–214.

40. See Spenser, *Faerie Queene,* books 2 and 3.

41. Spenser, *Variorum,* 10:89–90.

42. Anderson, "Antiquities."

43. Ralegh, *History,* 2.21.6.

44. See John Racin, *Sir Walter Ralegh as Historian* (Salzburg, 1972), part 2.

45. See chap. 3 in this volume.

46. Ralegh, *History,* 1.6.1.

47. Ibid., 2.13.6, citing Plutarch.

48. Ibid., 1.6.1.

49. Ibid., 2.14.1.

50. John Selden, introduction to annotations on Michael Drayton, *The Poly-Olbion* (London, 1622).

51. See chap. 2 in this volume.

52. John Selden, *Opera Omnia* (London, 1726), vol. 3, part 1, col. 103.

53. *Poly-Olbion,* book 1, p. 18.

54. Ibid., introduction; see also book 1, pp. 35–36.

55. Ibid., book 1, p. 36.

56. See, in general, *The Collected Works of Francis Bacon* (London, 1857–74), 8:439–44; and Judith H. Anderson, *Biographical Truth: The Representation of Historical Persons in Tudor-Stuart Writing* (New Haven, 1984), chaps. 9–10.

57. Bacon, *Works,* 8:439–40.

58. Ibid., 8:441.

59. Ibid.

60. Ibid., 8:442.

61. Other examples: John Rastell, *The Pastime of People* (London, 1529), ed. T. F. Dibdin (London, 1811), p. 7; Thomas Lanquet, *Epitome of Chronicles* (London, 1549), sig. Diii.

62. Bacon, *Works,* 9:266.

63. Ibid., 8:400–401.

64. Sidney, *Defence,* p. 15.

65. Ralegh, *History,* 2.21.6. Selden took a similar position in *History of Tithes,* in *Opera,* vol. 3, part 2, preface; also *Titles of Honor,* in *Opera,* vol. 3, part 1, preface. See also Barbara J. Schapiro, *Probability and Certainty in Seventeenth-Century England* (Princeton, 1983), pp. 149ff.; Michael McKeon, *The Origin of the English Novel 1600–1740* (Baltimore, 1987), pp. 52ff.

66. Spenser, *View,* p. 39.

67. Ibid.

68. Bacon, *Works,* 8:421.

69. Ibid., 8:423–25.

70. Ibid.

71. Sidney, *Defence,* p. 15.

72. Anderson, "Antiquities."

73. Bacon, *Works,* 8:453–54.

74. See chap. 3 in this volume.

75. See chap. 2 in this volume.

76. Bacon, *Works,* 13:77. See also 8:441. See also chap. 3 in this volume.

77. Bacon, *Works,* 13:80.

Index

Allegory, 24, 29; ancient wisdom and, 58–59; Bacon on, 127–28; euhemerism and, 15–16; history and, 15, 37–40; protector of gods, 14, 34, 42
American Indians, 5, 136, 140; "age of myth" and, 56–57; documentation for "cave myth," 62, 66, 77–79, 136, 143; euhemerism and, 28
André, Bernard, 86
Annius of Viterbo, 87, 106. *See also* Pseudo-Berosus
Ariosto, 124
Aristotle, 62, 65, 67, 72, 115, 120; *Poetics,* 115, 120, 122
Arthur, King, 73, 84–85, 90, 98–100, 105, 124, 129
Assembly of Gods, 21, 22
Augustine, Saint (Bishop of Hippo), 16, 18, 20, 21, 25, 29, 49, 51, 56

Bacon, Francis, 41, 42, 47, 67, 118, 121, 130, 142; on allegory, 39; faculty psychology and, 129; on invention, 33–34; on poetical history, 127–28; poets as euhemerizers, 119; on primitive mentality, 54–56
Bale, John, 86–87, 106
Banier, Antoine, 13–14, 40
Bardic legends: classical myths, relation to, 103; historical poetry and, 120–126; rejected by Selden, 103
Batman, Stephen, 25, 38
Bayle, Pierre, 139
Biblical scholarship: and the commentators, 40–41; comparative study in, 35–37; and Greek myths, 50–54. *See also* Biblical tradition
Biblical tradition, 11, 107, 110, 121, 125; and "cave myth," 61; and myth-history, 61; rationalization in, 40–41; and social evolution, 75–76; and state of nature, 80–81
Blackwell, Thomas, 40
Boccacio, 10
Bochart, Samuel, 35, 36, 52
Bodin, Jean, 26, 67, 69, 75, 96
Britons, 66, 79, 96, 106
Browne, Sir Thomas, 42
Brut, 84, 89
Brutus, 84, 85, 96, 100–102, 105, 106, 120, 124, 126

Caesar, Julius, 95
Camden, William, 8, 50, 88, 101; *Britannia,* 91, 94–95; caution in controversy, 94–95; hypothesis, use of, 95; on lost evidence, 102; rejection of legends, 101; skepticism about Arthur, 99; on state of nature, 82
Carpenter, Nathaniel, 66
Cartari, Vincenzo, 10, 25
Caxton, William, 84, 90; anachronism in, 17
Christine de Pisan, 17

Chronology: and biblical scholarship, 35–37, 50–54; and euhemerism, 15, 26, 35, 138; and literary scholarship, 50; scholarship concerning, 48–49; stages in history, 44, 49
Cicero: skepticism about the gods, 25, 29; on relation of poetry to history, 115
Clapham, John, 101
Colet, John, 115, 121
Conjecture: hypothesis, use of, 71, 92–93, 97; as interpretive device, 47, 137. *See also* Probability
Conti, Natale, 10, 36, 41
Cumberland, Richard, 139

Daniel, Samuel, 34, 133; British legends, rejection of, 101; as poetic historian, 128
Dares Frygius, 122
Decay of nature, myth of, 75, 76, 83, 111, 137
Dee, John, 100
Diodorus Siculus, 13, 62, 79
Drayton, Michael, 24, 25, 102, 103, 104, 111, 126, 133; caution about Arthur, 99–100; on poetic history, 128
Druids, 95, 96

Eden, Richard: on evolution of language, 69; on myths of aborigines, 57; on *tabula rasa,* 77
Elizabeth I, Queen, 86
Elizabethan Society of Antiquaries, 101
Elyot, Sir Thomas, 24, 27, 63
Erasmus, Desiderius, 63, 67
Euhemerism: ambivalence concerning, 26–28, 44–45; and "cave myth," 72–73; decline of, 134, 138, 142; as fact of history, 46, 140; and idolatry, 20–22, 48; medieval expressions of, 13–22 passim; rationalization of, 16–20, 41–43; skepticism concerning, 26–28
Euhemerus, 13
Eusebius, 29

Fontenelle, Bernard Le Bovier de, 139, 141
Fortescue, Sir John, 18
Fraunce, Abraham, 38

Gauls, 95, 106, 108
Genesis, 23, 61; biblical scholarship concerning, 40–41; giants, authority on, 107; on man's early history, 69–70; as poetic history, 121
Geoffrey of Monmouth, 50, 84, 86–87, 89, 91, 94, 101, 103, 106, 117
Golden Age, myth of, 5, 73–74, 83, 137
Golding, Arthur, 43
Goodman, Godfrey, 75
Goropius (Johan van Gorp), 107
Gower, John, 17

Hakewill, George, 54, 75
Harrington, John, 100
Harrison, William: on bardic tradition, 103, 120; on chronology, 48; on giants, 110–11
Henry VII, King, 86
Henry VIII, King, 85, 86, 89
Herbert of Cerbury, Lord, 29–30
Hermes Trismegistus, 21
Herodotus, 79
Hesiod, 19, 24, 30, 47, 50, 53, 55, 115, 116, 123
Heylyn, Peter, 70
Heywood, Thomas, 24, 119
Hieroglyphics, 55–57, 136
Higden, Ralph, 24, 35, 90, 107; skepticism, 20; theory of myth-history, 16–20
Historicization, 40, 42, 44
Hobbes, Thomas, 80–82, 141

Homer, 50, 53, 55, 103, 115, 116, 122, 123, 134
Hooker, Richard, 63, 70; on evolution of society, 67; on optimism, 77; rationalism of, 81; and state of nature, 80–81
Humanism, 8, 40, 56; and "cave myth," 61–63; and chronology, 35, 47; and historical truth, 116–17; medieval, 22; secular influence, 72
Hume, David, 141

Indians. *See* American Indians
Invention: and euhemerism, 31–34; gradualism, 31–34, 76–77
Isidore of Seville, 17, 19

James I, King, 100
Jones, Inigo, 112

Lafitau, Joseph François, 141
LeFèvre, Raoul, 17
Leland, John: on nonliterary evidence, 99; originality of, 96; versus Polydore Vergil, 99; skepticism about Arthur, 99
LeRoy, Louis, 11, 63, 67, 78; on Greek deities, 26; and invention, 72–73
Llhuyd, Humphrey, 96, 97–98: on linguistic conjecture, 99
Lloyd, Ludowick, 48
Locke, John, 80
Lucretius, 62, 71, 95
Lydgate, John, 17, 21
Lynche, Richard: *The Fountaine of Ancient Fiction,* 25

Malory, Sir Thomas, 18, 90
Mandeville, Sir John, 17
Merlin, 96, 103, 112
More, Sir Thomas, 88, 90, 117, 118, 122

Newton, Sir Isaac, 13, 139

Oral tradition, 97, 136
Ovid, 24, 38, 57
Owen, John, 36, 52

Palaephatus, 13; *De incredibilibus,* 41
Pecock, Reginald, 18, 48; on idolatry, 21–22
Phoenicians, 93, 108. *See also* Twyne, John
Plato, 42, 115; on poets, 115, 120
Pliny, 79, 108
Poets: as euhemerizers, 118–19; as myth-makers, 114–16
Polydore Vergil, 86, 88, 90, 98, 104; on the British History, 89; on invention, 32–33; scholarship of, 96
Price, Sir John, 99–100, 103; scholarship of, 96–99
Primitive mentality: and "age of myth," 55–57; and "cave myth," 67; in Enlightenment thought, 141; and wisdom of the ancients, 57
Probability: in poetic history, 122; and historical interpretation, 124, 131, 137
Pseudo-Berosus, 57, 87, 106
Purchas, Samuel, 27
Puttenham, George, 50, 62, 69, 78, 123, 128; on American Indians, 68; on euhemerism, 31–32; on "poesie historical," 121–22; on poets as euhemerizers, 118

Quarrel of Ancients and Moderns, 34, 54, 57, 75

Ralegh, Sir Walter, 24, 35, 36, 65, 92, 124; on American Indians, 78; on chronology, 51; on euhemerism, 28–29; on giants, 107–10; on poetry as history, 125–26; on probability, 129; secular tendency, 72

Rastell, John, 86, 90, 99, 191
Ripa, Cesare, 10
Ross, Alexander, 36, 38, 109
Royal Society, 112, 133

Salter, George, 102
Sandys, George, 24, 36, 38, 41, 50, 121
Scaliger, Joseph Justus, 35, 50, 110; *De emendatione temporum,* 48
Selden, John, 104, 111, 124, 128; on Arthurian legends, 100, 102; on bardic tradition, 103, 126; on giants, 111; on lost evidence, 102, 103; on poetical history, 126–27; skepticism about legendary history, 25, 30
Shuckford, Samuel, 13, 139
Sidney, Sir Philip, 119, 128, 129; on poetry versus history, 122–23; on poets as interpreters of past, 130–31
Skepticism: anti-Galfridean, 88, 90, 97; and decline of euhemerism, 101–2; in England, 40, 47; about euhemerism, 26–27, 30; medieval expressions of, 18–20; slow progress of, 42
Smith, Sir Thomas, 53, 62, 67, 75; on invention, 33
Social evolution: awareness of, 136; and biblical tradition, 69–72, 75; and "cave myth," 67–75; and Enlightenment thought, 141; and euhemerism, 33–35, 72–73; and Golden Age, 73–75; language as a factor in, 68; and optimism, 77–78
Speed, John, 79
Spenser, Edmund, 39, 79, 100; ambivalence about poetry as history, 131; on bardic tradition, 103, 120, 124, 125; on historical poetry, 123–25; on poets as euhemerizers, 118; on probability, 129–30; on truth in legend, 102
Starkey, Thomas, 66, 67, 74, 77, 80; on "cave myth," 62–65
State of nature: relation to "cave myth," 79–82
Stillingfleet, Edward, 30, 48, 55, 71, 75; on chronology, 36–37; on Greek myths in relation to "Scripture History," 53–54, 75; on poets as euhemerizers, 119
Stonehenge, 108
Strabo, 53

Tacitus, 96
Taliesin, 96, 103
Tasso, 124
Thales, 52
Trevisa, John, 90
Twyne, John, 63, 88, 95, 103; on Britons, 79; *De rebus Albionicis, Britannicis atque Anglicis,* 91; on giants, 107–9, 110; on gods, 27; hypothesis, use of, 92–94; on use of myth, 104

Varro, 19, 25, 50, 51, 54, 95, 104; on periodization, 47–49
Vico, Giambattista, 139
Virgil, 122, 124
Vitruvius, 62
Vives, Juan Luis, 11, 33, 41, 63, 67, 91, 92; on euhemerism, 27–28; on Olympiads, 47, 49; skepticism about the gods, 14–15; on social evolution, 67–68; on truth in poetry, 116–17

Warburton, William, 13, 139
Warner, William, 24, 99
Webbe, William, 68
Wethamsted, John, 90
William of Newburgh, 87
William the Conqueror, 111
Wills, Richard: *De re poetica,* 50
Wilson, Sir Thomas, 63–70

About the Author

Arthur B. Ferguson is Professor of History Emeritus at Duke University. His publications include *The Indian Summer of English Chivalry: Studies in the Decline and Transformation of Chivalric Idealism*, *The Articulate Citizen and the English Renaissance*, *Clio Unbound: Perception of the Social and Cultural Past in Renaissance England*, and *The Chivalric Tradition in Renaissance England*.

Library of Congress Cataloging-in-Publication Data

Ferguson, Arthur B.

Utter antiquity : perception of prehistory in Renaissance England / by Arthur B. Ferguson.

p. cm. — (Duke monographs in medieval and Renaissance studies ; no. 13)

Includes bibliographical references and index.

ISBN 0-8223-1275-1

1. Anthropology, Prehistoric—England—History. 2. Renaissance—England. 3. Legends—History and criticism. 4. Mythology.

I. Title. II. Series.

GN761.F47 1993

936.2—dc20 92-12470

CIP